The Ṣalāh of RASŪLULLĀH

صَلَّى ٱللَّٰهُ عَلَيْهِ وَسَلَّمَ

In the name of Allāh, Most Gracious, Most Merciful.

All praise be to Allāh, Lord of the worlds,
and peace and blessings be upon His Messenger Muḥammad,
Mercy to the Worlds.

The Ṣalāh of RASŪLULLĀH

ﷺ

TRANSLATION OF
CHAHL ḤADĪTH MASĀ'IL-I-NAMĀZ

A Compilation of Forty Authentic Ḥadīths on Ṣalāh, with Arabic Text, Translation and Brief Commentary

SHAYKH ZAHOOR AHMAD AL-HUSAYNI

Translated by
MUHAMMAD YASIR AL-HANAFI

NASAFI PUBLICATIONS

ISBN 978-1-9160347-0-9

Published by:
Nasafi Publications
Nasafipublications@mail.com

Author	Shaykh Zahoor Ahmad Al-Husayni
Translator	Muhammad Yasir al-Hanafi
Editor	Javed Iqbal
Sub-Editor	Muhammad Sahil
Cover Design & Typesetting	Javed Iqbal
Printed by	Mega Printing, Istanbul, Turkey
	export@mega.com.tr

TRANSLATOR'S DEDICATION

For my beloved younger brother:
Mawlānā Mohammad Atif, whose piety was an example for me, and whose company I miss greatly.

May Allah have mercy on him and elevate his status.
May Allah reunite us, along with the rest of the Ummah, in His Gardens of Paradise. Āmīn.

TRANSLITERATION KEY

ا	', a, ā
ب	b
ت	t
ث	th
ج	j
ح	ḥ
خ	kh
د	d
ذ	dh
ر	r
ز	z
س	s
ش	sh
ص	ṣ
ض	ḍ
ط	ṭ
ظ	ẓ
ع	ʿ, ʿā, ʿī, ʿū
غ	gh
ف	f
ق	q
ك	k
ل	l
م	m
ن	n
و	w, ū, u
ه	h
ي	y, ī, i

ﷺ used following the mention of the Prophet Muḥammad, translated as, "May Allāh bless and send peace upon him".

(*from left to right*) used following the mention of a male Companion, female Companion, two Companions and more than two Companions respectively, translated as, "May Allāh be pleased with him/her/them."

"May Allāh have mercy on him."

CONTENTS

Foreword

Shaykh al-Ḥadīth Mawlānā Salimullah Khan ﷺ

Ḥaḍrat Mawlānā Zahoor Ahmad al-Husayni (may his shade be lengthened) has very skillfully compiled forty authentic ḥadīths on ṣalāh, with the Arabic text, Urdu translation and necessary explanation.

With respect to the narrations and their explanation, the content is very comprehensive and substantial, such that this concise work will give readers sufficient knowledge on every topic, freeing them from the need for lengthy books. This book is worthy of being added to the syllabi of educational institutes at the intermediate level. If people from all backgrounds, scholars and students alike, take benefit from this book in their daʿwah work, preservation work and lectures, it can, *in-shā'-Allāh*, close the doors to objections against the Ḥanafī school of thought.

May Allāh Most High accept the efforts of the compiler and enable him to do more beneficial work. *Āmīn.*

(Mawlānā) Salimullah Khan (ﷺ)
Head of Wifāq al-Madāris al-ʿArabiyyah, Pakistan,
Shaykh al-ḥadīth and principal, Jāmiʿah Fārūqiyyah, Karachi.

20 SHAʿBĀN 1436 AH | 8 JUNE 2015

The Prophet ﷺ said:
"The first matter that the slave will be brought to account for on the Day of Judgment is ṣalāh. If it is sound, then the rest of his deeds will be sound. But if it is corrupt, the rest of his deeds will be corrupt."

Ṭabarānī

Foreword

Shaykh al-Ḥadīth Mawlānā Mufti Musa Badat
(*ḥafiẓahullāh*)

We praise Allāh, and send blessings and peace upon the Prophet ﷺ, whereafter we say: In the famous ḥadīth, it is mentioned: "Whoever memorises forty ḥadīths regarding matters of the religion for my Ummah, Allāh ﷻ will resurrect him as a jurist, and I will be an intercessor and witness for him on the Day of Judgement."[1]

To attain this virtue, scholars of the religion compiled forty ḥadīth collections (*arbaʿūn*) on different topics. One of the links in this series is Mawlānā Zahoor Ahmad al-Husayni's book: *Chahl Ḥadith Masā'il-i-Namaz*, in which he has proven ṣalāh according to the Ḥanafī school from authentic ḥadīths, and removed the misconception of some people that ṣalāh according to the Ḥanafī school is not established from authentic ḥadīths.

The reality is that this misconception is based on unawareness of the ḥadīth sciences. Authentic ḥadiths are not confined to Bukhārī and Muslim alone. It is understood from studying the books of ḥadīth principles that authentic ḥadīths are of seven types, which exist in various ḥadīth compilations. After authentic ḥadīths, there are also sound (*ḥasan*) ḥadīths from which religious matters are established. The *sunan* compilations are filled with such narrations. Juristic matters are proven

1 *Sharaf Aṣḥāb al-Ḥadīth* (29, 31).

from the Qur'ān, Sunnah and consensus (*ijmāʿ*); they are not separate from them.

Mawlānā Yasir (may Allah protect him), through ability from Allāh, has translated this book into English with great effort.

May Allāh accept this endeavour of his, and make it immensely beneficial for the Ummah and a provision for us all in the hereafter. *Āmīn.*

The servant (Muftī) Musa Badat (may he be forgiven)
8 ṢAFAR 1440 AH

Foreword

Shaykh al-Ḥadīth Mawlānā Muhammad Saleem Dhorat
(*ḥafiẓahullāh*)

Differences in matters related to Islāmic jurisprudence (*fiqh*) have always been and shall remain an integral part of academic discussion between the honourable ʿulamāʾ. These differences arise due to a number of factors, including variations in the principles adopted in the science of tafsīr, ḥadīth and fiqh, and in the interpretation of Qurʾānic and ḥadīth texts.

These factors can only be truly understood and appreciated by the rightly guided ʿulamāʾ of the ummah. Historically these differences did not become a means of hatred and animosity between the sincere ʿulamāʾ, let alone the general public, nor did they seek to enforce their opinions on others.

Ḥāfiẓ al-Dhahabī ﷀ has quoted Imām Abū Mūsā al-Ṣadafī ﷀ saying:

ما رأيت أعقل من الشافعي، ناظرته يوما في مسألة، ثم افترقنا، ولقيني، فأخذ بيدي، ثم قال: يا أبا موسى، ألا يستقيم أن نكون إخوانا وإن لم نتفق في مسألة؟ قلت: هذا يدل على كمال عقل هذا الإمام، وفقه نفسه.

I have not seen anyone more intelligent than Imām Shāfiʿī ﷀ. One day I debated with him regarding a ruling and then we parted. He then met me and took hold of my hand and said: O Abū Mūsā! Can we not remain brothers, even if we disagree on a ruling?'

Ḥāfiẓ al-Dhahabī ﵀ thereafter writes: 'This shows the excellence of this Imām's intelligence and his deep understanding."[2]

The existence of such differences within matters of *fiqh* intuitively highlights, inter alia, the necessity of following an imām from the four major schools of fiqh: Ḥanafī; Mālikī; Shāfi'ī; and Ḥanbalī, to safeguard one from delving into intricate areas of Islām for which the majority are not qualified.

Furthermore, following any one of these four great Imāms simply means to follow the commands of Allāh Ta'ālā, as taught to us by Rasūllullāh ﷺ, according to their deep understanding. May Allāh Ta'ālā reward them and shower His mercies upon them.

It is unfortunate that in recent history, certain groups and individuals have become intolerant of differences in matters of fiqh, straying from the path of the pious predecessors and advocating their fiqhī opinions as the only valid viewpoint, thus becoming a cause of controversy. Such divergence continues to create confusion and casts doubt within the hearts of the followers of these four Imāms, who continue to represent the overwhelming majority of the Ummah.

The book at hand, *The Ṣalāh of Rasūlullāh* ﷺ is an English translation of the book *Chahl Ḥadīth* compiled by Mawlānā Zahoor Ahmad al-Husayni (*ḥafiẓahullāh*). The original Urdu text is a compilation of forty authentic ḥadīths, with brief commentary, substantiating the manner of performing ṣalāh according to the fiqh of Imām Abū Ḥanīfah ﵀.

The content presented truly affords a believer the opportunity to practice upon the order of Rasūllullāh ﷺ:

صلّوا كما رأيتموني أصلي

2 *Siyar A'lām Al-Nubalā'*, 10:15-16.

Perform ṣalāh as you see me perform ṣalāh.[3]

Mawlānā (*ḥafiẓahullāh*) has meticulously chosen these forty authentic narrations, from the many, and together with substantiating the *sunnah* method of ṣalāh according to the Ḥanafī school of thought, attained the virtue of propagating forty ḥadīths to the ummah. Mawlānā (*ḥafiẓahullāh*) is a well-versed author of many academic books who continuously remains in the service of knowledge. May Allāh Taʿālā increase him in his knowledge and practice, and accept his efforts. *Āmīn.*

Appreciating the value of this book for the English-speaking audience, a very active and passionate young ʿālim, my dear Mawlānā Muhammad Yasir al-Hanafi (*zīda majduhū*), has translated it into lucid English. *Inshā'Allāh*, this translation will be a means of alleviating confusion, and strengthening confidence and trust in the great Imāms ﵏.

May Allāh Taʿālā accept this translation and grant Mawlānā Muhammad Yasir the ability to produce many more beneficial works. *Āmīn.*

(Mawlānā) Muḥammad Saleem Dhorat
Islāmic Da'wah Academy
Leicester

1 MUḤARRAM 1440 | 11 SEPTEMBER 2018

3 *Bukhāri* (6008).

Indeed, mankind was created anxious:
When evil touches him, impatient,
And when good touches him, withholding [of it],
Except the observers of prayer -
Those who are constant in their prayer.

Qur'ān 70:10-23

Foreword

Muftī Abdur-Rahman ibn Yusuf Mangera
(*ḥafiẓahullāh*)

In the name of Allāh, Most Gracious Most Merciful

All praise is to Allāh, Lord of the Worlds, the focus of our devotion and the bestower of abundant bounties upon His creation. Peace and blessings be upon his chosen Prophet, who showed us how to devote ourselves to Allāh, how to pray to Him and the secrets of having our prayers accepted by Him.

Thereafter, upon all those who sincerely expounded on his teachings, conveyed them to successive generations, and defended them from the corruption, interpolation, misinterpretation, misunderstanding and obfuscation that crept into them from time to time.

Over the centuries, there may have been healthy debates between the various schools of Islamic law (*madhhabs*) about the way the Messenger of Allāh ﷺ prayed, but they hardly lead to people considering one another corrupted, deviated or out of the fold of Islam. Unfortunately, the attitude of insisting on a single way of prayer, and considering all other ways to be deviant (even though they are evidenced from the Qur'ān and Sunna and represented by the vast majority of the Muslim Umma) surfaced in the last few decades, coming to a head in the Western World about two decades ago.

One of the main books that could be held responsible for much of this confusion was Shaykh Nāṣir al-Dīn al-Albānī's *The Prophet's Prayer Described* (1993).

In line with timeless scholarly custom, scholars stood up to clarify the position of the Ḥanafī prayer, which generally suffered the brunt of these attacks. Several satisfying works were produced on the defence of it, demonstrating beyond doubt its rooting in the Qur'ān and Prophetic Sunna. Hence, this writer's *Fiqh al-Imam* (1996), Shaykh Abu Yusuf Riyadh ul Haq's *The Salah of a Believer in the Quran and Sunnah* (1998), translations of Imām Muḥammad al-Shaybānī's *Kitāb al-Āthār* of Imām Abū Ḥanīfah (2006) and Imām Muḥammad al-Nīmawī's *Āthār as-Sunan* (2012), along with several other related books, were produced and appreciated widely.

Since then, with the grace of Allāh, the confusion and strife caused by such non-*madhhabī* objectors, was for the most part controlled and dealt with. Many of the same group of objectors and their followers learned to tolerate, if not accept, the acceptability of praying according to one of the *madhhabs*. An ideology established to criticise others and consider them deviant cannot be sustainable.

In hindsight, it is very clear that what they were really calling to was a fifth *madhhab*, and not a direct and sincere following of the Qur'an and Sunna, as was the fanciful claim. The proof of this is evident. Hypothetically, if someone were to take directly from the primary sources, the Qur'ān and Sunna, but were to end up preferring ḥadīths and ruling that the main scholars of this group did not prefer, it would also be condemned. So it was not really a direct return to the primary sources they were calling to, but rather the blind following of their scholars' conclusions; in other words a new modern, fifth *madhhab*.

Why anyone would give up the tested and tried authority and relevance of the four existing *madhhabs*, for a set of new ideas built upon the opposition of nearly thirteen hundred years of solid scholarship, is indeed baffling.

Unfortunately, there still remains a negligible minority among them who still aimlessly bang the same drums and revive the same debate in some circles. Therefore, this remarkable collection of forty ḥadīths on the subject of prayer, which is in your hands, has been ably translated into English to put the matter to rest, once and for all. Both the compiler and translator are competent scholars. The forty ḥadīths here have been further substantiated by numerous ḥadīth authorities and commentators, including a number of non-*madhhabī* scholars, which provides a unique angle to this subject. The compiler's profound erudition, deep knowledge and extensive scope of resources is clearly displayed in this work.

We pray to Allāh to allow it to benefit many, and make it a means of them enjoying their devotion and worship free of confusions and doubts. *Āmīn.*

(Muftī) Abdur-Rahman ibn Yusuf Mangera
Whitethread Institute, London

RABĪʿ AL-ĀKHIR 1440 | DECEMBER 2018

The Prophet ﷺ said:

"If there was a river at one's door in which he bathed five times a day, what do you say: Will any dirt remain on him?" They said, "No dirt will remain on him." He replied, "That is the example of the five ṣalāhs; Allāh removes sins through them."

Bukhārī, Muslim

Translator's Note

بسم الله الرحمن الرحيم.

الحمد لله ربّ العٰلمين، والصّلاة والسّلام على سيّدنا ونبيّنا محمّد وعلى آله وصحبه أجمعين. أمّا بعد:

Undoubtedly, the most important thing after īmān (faith) in the life of a believer, is ṣalāh. Allāh Most High says: "Success is really attained by the believers, who concentrate their attention in humbleness when offering ṣalāh (prayers)."[4] Sayyidunā ʿUmar ﷺ narrates that the Messenger of Allāh ﷺ said: "The place of ṣalāh in religion is like the place of the head in the body."[5] If a person has a limb missing, such as a hand, or it does not function properly due to a disability, the body will still function. However, there is no possibility of life without the head.

Hence, it is not out of place to say salvation in the Hereafter (*ākhirah*) is dependent on the completion and perfection of the five daily ṣalāhs. The Messenger of Allāh ﷺ said: "The first of man's deeds for which he will be called to account on the Day of Resurrection will be his ṣalāh. If it is found to be perfect, he will be safe and successful; but if it is incomplete, he will be unfortunate and a loser. If any shortcoming is found in the obligatory ṣalāh, the Glorious and Exalted Lord will command:

---

4 Qur'an, 23:1-2.

5 *Al-Muʿjam al-Awsaṭ* (2292).

'See if My slave has offered any voluntary ṣalāh, so that the obligatory ṣalāh may be made up by it.' Then the rest of his actions will be treated in the same manner."[6] May Allāh enable us all to offer our ṣalāh with perfection and punctuality until our last day in this temporary life. *Āmīn.*

This work is a translation of Mawlānā Zahoor Ahmad al-Husayni's Urdu book *Chahl Ḥadīth Masā'il Namāz*, a collection of forty ḥadīths pertaining to this important topic of ṣalāh. These forty ḥadīths are evidences for the *sunnah* ṣalāh of the Prophet ﷺ, as understood by the Ḥanafī jurists (*fuqahā'*). Mawlānā Zahoor (may Allāh preserve him) is an erudite scholar whom Allāh has gifted with the prowess of proficiently writing academic works in defence of various aspects of the religion, especially the Ḥanafī school. Thus, this book, as well as his other works, illustrates his profound knowledge. He has succinctly gathered the evidences for ṣalāh, with the Arabic text of the ḥadīth, its translation and brief explanation, and students of knowledge and scholars alike will find it beneficial, *in-shā'-Allāh.*

The purpose of translating this comprehensive work is not to criticise or fault any other method of ṣalāh, but rather to educate and instil confidence in the masses who follow the Ḥanafī school that their ṣalāh is also according to the method of our beloved Prophet ﷺ. The four schools of jurisprudence, Ḥanāfī, Mālikī, Shāfiʿī and Ḥanbalī, are all based upon the Qur'ān and Sunnah, and for any sane Muslim to claim otherwise is absurd.

Since many of the attacks on the Ḥanafī method of ṣalāh are from our non-muqallid brothers, a relative minority within the Muslim Ummah, Mawlānā Zahoor has cited non-muqallid scholars in authenticating most of the narrations in this book.

6 Tirmidhī (413).

The purpose of quoting them is to establish evidence against the non-muqallids, not that these scholars are the foremost authorities in the ḥadīth sciences. In this work, we have highlighted each non-muqallid scholar with an asterisk in the first instance they have been cited.

In addition to this, I would like to remind the reader that the evidences for the Ḥanafī method of ṣalāh are not limited to these forty ḥadīths. There are many other narrations from major books of ḥadīth that qualify as substantial evidences for the Ḥanafī method of ṣalāh. However, Mawlānā Zahoor has sufficed upon forty for a certain reason which he has explained in his preface.

Finally, I earnestly thank my dear parents and family; the esteemed ʿulamā' who kindly wrote forewords to this translation, namely my respected teacher, Muftī Musa Badat; the esteemed shaykh, Mawlānā Salim Dhorat; and Muftī Abdur Raḥmān Mangera. I also thank my dear friends Mawlānā Sahil, Usamah Muttakin, and Abu Humayd for their continued support; Muftī Javed Iqbal who edited this book with great effort; and all who helped bring this publication to light. Most importantly, I thank Mawlānā Zahoor Ahmad al-Husayni for granting permission to translate his work.

May Allāh bless them and their families with the best in both worlds, and may He accept this humble endeavour and makes it a means of guidance for all. *Āmīn.*

Muhammad Yasir Al-Hanafi

TUESDAY 27 RAMAḌĀN 1439 AH 12 JUNE 2018

ʿALLĀMAH KHALID MAHMOOD'S COMMENDATION

The ṣalāh of the Prophet ﷺ (in which he instructed: 'pray as you have seen me pray', as reported by Imām al-Bukhārī) can only be told to us by those who witnessed the Prophet ﷺ offering ṣalāh. To solve this matter, the pious predecessors (*Salaf*) explained the methodology of the Sunnah. Those who have adopted the way of the Sunnah have named themselves Ahl al-Sunnah, not Ahl al-Ḥadīth. This book is a valuable asset to the ṣalāh of the Ahl al-Sunnah.[7]

7 I was fortunate to show this work to ʿAllāmah Khalid Mahmood (may Allāh preserve him) a few times. He read it from several places and was pleased with the work - and all praise is for Allāh. Despite his being advanced in age, he provided some valuable suggestions, which demonstrate his sagacity even at this age. He also dictated the few words above to add to this work. (*Translator's Note*).

Preface

بِسْمِ اللهِ الرَّحْمٰنِ الرَّحِيْمِ.

نَحْمَدُهُ وَنُصَلِّيْ وَنُسَلِّمُ عَلَى رَسُوْلِهِ الْكَرِيْمِ، أَمَّا بَعْدُ:

The Leader of Both Worlds ﷺ said:

مَنْ حَفِظَ عَلَى أُمَّتِيْ أَرْبَعِيْنَ حَدِيْثًا مِنْ أَمْرِ دِيْنِهَا بَعَثَهُ اللهُ فَقِيْهًا، وَكُنْتُ لَهُ يَوْمَ الْقِيَامَةِ شَافِعًا وَّشَهِيْدًا.

> Whoever memorises forty ḥadīths regarding matters of the religion for my Ummah, Allāh ﷻ will resurrect him as a jurist, and I will be an intercessor and witness for him on the Day of Judgement.[8]

To attain this virtue, many reputable scholars compiled books of forty ḥadīths on different topics. Amongst the books of ḥadīth, many compilations under the forty-ḥadīth (*arbaʿūn*) category can be found.[9]

---

8 *Mishkāt al-Maṣābīḥ* (258)

9 Admittedly, ḥadīth experts have declared it a weak hadīth despite its numerous chains of transmission. However, Imām Nawawī رحمه الله enumerates many imāms who compiled forty-ḥadīth collections: ʿAbdullāh ibn al-Mubārak (d. 181 AH), Muḥammad ibn Aslam al-Ṭusī (d. 242 AH), Ḥasan ibn Sufyān al-Nasawī (d. 303 AH), Muhammad ibn Ḥusayn al-Ājurrī (d. 360 AH), Abū Bakr al-Iṣbahānī (d. 366 AH), ʿAlī ibn ʿUmar al-Dāraquṭnī (d. 385 AH), Al-Ḥākim (d. 405 AH), Abū Nuʿaym (d. 430 AH), Abū ʿAbd al-Raḥmān al-Sulamī (d. 412 AH), Abū Saʿīd al-Mālīnī (d. 412 AH), Abū ʿUthmān al-Ṣābūnī (d. 449 AH), ʿAbdullāh

This compilation of forty ḥadīths is pertaining to a very important foundation of the religion, ṣalāh, and consists of authentic (*ṣaḥīh*) and sound (*ḥasan*) narrations. Anyone who memorises and propagates these forty ḥadīths will be entitled to this reward, *in-shā'-Allāh*, and be fortunate to perform an act of worship as important as ṣalāh according to the Sunnah.

It should be noted that in this compilation of ḥadīth regarding the rulings of ṣalāh, the ḥadīths have been presented as evidence, and the statements of the imāms of the Ummah as explanation to the ḥadīths.

The Ḥanafī school is a compilation of juristic issues that have been deduced from the Qur'ān and Sunnah. Hence, this book consists of those forty ḥadīths which are evidences for forty issues compiled by the Ḥanafī jurists ﷺ.

A substantial number of ḥadīths have been taken from *Ṣaḥīḥ al-Bukhārī* and *Ṣaḥīḥ Muslim*. As for those ḥadīths that are not in the the abovementioned works, their authenticity or soundness has been reported from reputable ḥadīth scholars (*muḥaddithūn*). In addition to this, narrations of Rasūlullāh ﷺ, the Ṣaḥābah ﷺ and the Tābiʿūn ﷺ have also been mentioned as further support to these ḥadīths.

Non-muqallids[10] have opened the door to rejection of

---

ibn Muḥammad al-Anṣārī (d. 481 AH), Abū Bakr al-Bayhaqī (d. 458 AH) and many others.

In the foreword to his *Arbaʿūn* compilation, Imām Nawawī ﷺ says: "I sought good from Allāh Most High in collecting forty hadīths, following these renowned imāms and hadīth experts (*ḥuffāẓ*) of Islam. Scholars are agreed on the permissibility of acting on a weak narration related to virtues of actions. Despite this, my reliance is not on this hadīth [only], but rather on his saying in authentic narrations, 'The present among you should convey to the absent' and his saying, 'May Allāh keep radiant one who hears my saying, memorises it and then conveys it as he heard it.'"

10 People who do not follow one of the four schools of jurisprudence.

ḥadīths by objecting to some of the ḥadīths used here. Therefore, statements of senior non-muqallid scholars have been cited in authenticating these ḥadīths and elaborating the issues as evidence against this group.

Since non-muqallids have rejected *taqlīd*[11], regarding themselves as opponents to the muqallids of the four great Imāms (Abū Ḥanīfah, Mālik, Shāfiʿī and Aḥmad ibn Ḥanbal ﵏), and are proud over rejecting *taqlīd* too, they have been given the title non-muqallid. They do not adhere to the methodology of the predecessors when reconciling between differing ḥadīths or giving preference, but rather take the path of rejection, thus opening the doors to ḥadīth rejection. This is why it is incorrect to refer to them as Ahl-i-Ḥadīth (i.e., people of ḥadīth).

With respect to compiling and organising juristic rulings derived from the Qur'ān and Sunnah into chapters, Allāh ﷻ took the most service from Ḥanafī jurists (*fuqahā'*) ﵏. For this reason, brief introductions about the erudite Imām Abū Ḥanīfah ﵀ and the Ḥanafī school have been included at the beginning of this book. These introductions were written by my honourable brother, Mawlānā Nithar Ahmad al-Husayni (may his blessings remain).

Three editions of this ḥadīth compilation have been published thus far, and Allāh ﷻ has blessed it with acceptance amongst scholars and laymen alike. All praises are due to Allāh for this.

Before you is the fourth edition of this book, with many extra beneficial points. In this latest edition, objections raised against a number of ḥadīths by some non-muqallids (such as Zubair Ali Zai) have also been briefly answered.

May Allah ﷻ accept this compilation of ḥadīth, make it a means of forgiveness for the writer and his parents, a means

11 Following one of the four schools.

of high ranks for his teachers and elders, and a means of rectification (of actions) for the believers. *Āmīn.*

اٰمين، بجاه النبيِّ الكريم، صلى الله عليه وعلَى آله وأصحابه وسلّم.

The lowly: (Mawlānā) Zahoor Ahmad al-Husayni (may Allāh forgive him)

22 RABĪʿ AL-AWWAL 1436 AH | 14 JANUARY 2015
Gillingham, Kent
United Kingdom

Imām Abū Ḥanīfah ﷺ

بِسْمِ اللهِ الرَّحْمٰنِ الرَّحِيْمِ.

اَلْحَمْدُ لِلّٰهِ رَبِّ الْعَالَمِيْنَ، والصَّلٰوةُ والسَّلَامُ عَلَى سَيِّدِ الْمُرْسَلِيْنَ،

أَمَّا بَعْدُ:

The light of the Ummah (*Sirāj al-Ummah*), Imām of the ḥadīth scholars (*muḥaddithūn*), well-wisher of the ummah, the great Imām Abū Ḥanīfah al-Nu'mān ibn Thābit ibn Zūṭā ﷺ was born in the year 80 AH (699 AD) in Kufa, the centre of Islamic learning in Iraq.

At the time, Kufa was not only a centre of knowledge for Iraq, but rather for the whole world. Sayyidunā 'Umar al-Fārūq ﷺ founded the city of Kufa in the year 17 AH upon the conquest of Iraq, and he sent Sayyidunā 'Abdullāh ibn Mas'ūd ﷺ to Kufa to overlook affairs of Islamic learning. Kufa was inhabited by great scholars. Apart from Sayyidunā 'Abdullāh ibn Mas'ud ﷺ, leading Ṣaḥābah, such as Sayyidunā Sa'd ibn Abī Waqqāṣ, Sayyidunā Ḥudhaifah ibn al-Yamān, Sayyidunā 'Ammār ibn Yāsir, Sayyidunā Salmān al-Fārisī and Sayyidunā Abū Mūsā al-Ash'arī ﷺ lived in Kufa. Kufa was home to fifteen hundred Ṣaḥābah of Rasūlullāh ﷺ, as well as the hub of their academic activities. The Door to Knowledge (*bāb al-'ilm*)[12], Sayyidunā 'Alī al-Murtaḍā ﷺ made Kufa the capital of the Islamic caliphate, due to it being

12 As reported by Ḥākim in *al-Mustadrak* (4637).

renowned for its knowledge, and thus Kufa's reputation was enhanced even further.

Imām Ibn Taymiyyah ﵀ said:

وإِنَّمَا ظَهَرَ عِلْمُ عَلِيٍّ وَفِقْهُهُ فِي الْكُوْفَةِ.

The knowledge of ʿAlī ﵁ and his jurisprudence (*fiqh*) became apparent in Kufa.[13]

Imām Abū Ḥanīfah ﵀ was brought up in this environment of knowledge in Kufa, whereby he attained knowledge from great Ṣaḥābah, Tābiʿūn, jurists (*fuqahā'*) and ḥadīth scholars (*muḥaddithūn*). The great ḥadīth scholar, Ḥāfiẓ Ibn Kathīr ﵀ (d. 774 AH) mentioned that some ḥadīth scholars (*muḥaddithūn*) have clearly stated that Imām Abū Ḥanīfah ﵀ narrated ḥadīths from seven honourable Ṣaḥābah ﵃.[14]

Ḥāfiẓ ʿAbd al-Qādir al-Qurashī ﵀ (d. 775 AH) has enumerated those seven Ṣaḥābah as follows:

1. Sayyidunā ʿAbdullāh ibn Unays ﵁;
2. Sayyidunā ʿAbdullāh ibn Jaz' al-Zubaydī ﵁;
3. Sayyidunā Anas ibn Mālik ﵁;
4. Sayyidunā Jābir ibn ʿAbdullāh ﵁;
5. Sayyidunā Maʿqil ibn Yasār ﵁;
6. Sayyidunā Wāthilah ibn al-Athqaʿ ﵁;
7. Sayyidah ʿĀ'ishah bint Ajrad ﵂.[15]

Apart from the scholars of Kufa, Imām Abū Ḥanīfah ﵀ acquired knowledge from many reputable scholars of various cities, such as Basra, and especially from the scholars of the two noble cities, Makkah al-Mukarramah and al-Madīnah al-Munawwarah.

---

13 *Minhāj al-Sunnah*, 3:137.

14 *Al-Bidāyah wa al-Nihāyah*, 7:86.

15 *Al-Jawāhir al-Muḍī'ah*, 1:28.

The Imām had performed ḥajj fifty times, and in every journey, he acquired knowledge. In that era, one of the means of acquiring knowledge was to travel for ḥajj. He had performed his first ḥajj at the age of seventeen alongside his father ﷺ, and therein he had the honour of listening to ḥadīths directly from the ṣaḥābī of Rasūlullāh ﷺ, Sayyidunā ʿAbdullāh ibn al-Ḥārith ﷺ.

The aforementioned seven Ṣaḥābah are those from whom Imām Abū Ḥanīfah ﷺ directly heard ḥadīths. As for those Ṣaḥābah from whom Imām Abū Ḥanīfah ﷺ had narrated ḥadīth indirectly, they are many.

In addition to this, Imām Abū Ḥanīfah ﷺ acquired knowledge from four thousand Tābiʿūn and Tabʿ Tābiʿīn.[16]

Imām Khalaf ibn Ayyūb ﷺ said:

صَارَ الْعِلْمُ مِنَ اللهِ تَعَالَى إِلَى مُحَمَّدٍ ﷺ، ثُمَّ صَارَ إِلَى أَصْحَابِهِ ﷺ، ثُمَّ صَارَ إِلَى التَّابِعِيْنَ ﷺ، ثُمَّ صَارَ إِلَى أَبِيْ حَنِيْفَةَ ﷺ وَأَصْحَابِهِ ﷺ، فَمَنْ شَاءَ فَلْيَرْضَ، وَمَنْ شَاءَ فَلْيَسْخُطْ.

> Knowledge was given by Allāh ﷻ to Muḥammad ﷺ, then it went to his Ṣaḥābah, then it went to the Tābiʿūn, and then it went to Abū Ḥanīfah ﷺ and his students. Whoever wishes can be pleased, and whoever wishes can be displeased.[17]

When Imām Abū Ḥanīfah ﷺ took his post as a teacher, students from all over the world came to study by him. In his lessons, the issues that were derived from the Qur'ān and Sunnah were referred to as the science of jurisprudence (*fiqh*) and these lessons became known as lessons of jurisprudence (*fiqh*). These lessons were the final stages of students'

16 The generation after the Tābiʿūn.

17 *Tārīkh Baghdād*, 13:336.

studies, and was for those who had mastered the sciences of the Arabic language, Arabic literature, ḥadīth and Qur'ānic exegesis (*tafsīr*).

The students of Imām Abū Ḥanīfah ﷺ would study how to deduce rulings, after they had attained knowledge of ḥadīth from the ḥadīth scholars (*muḥaddithūn*). These lessons of jurisprudence (*fiqh*) were considered superior to the lesson of ḥadīth, Qur'ānic exegesis (*tafsīr*) and the other sciences. Hence, a ḥadīth scholar (*muḥaddith*), exegete (*mufassir*), grammarian, and so forth, would be experts in their own respective fields, whereas a jurist (*faqīh*) would be an expert in all Islamic sciences.

This can be understood from an anecdote narrated by Imām ʿAbdullāh ibn ʿAmr ﷺ: Once, the great ḥadīth scholar (*muḥaddith*), Imām Aʿmash ﷺ, and Imām Abū Ḥanīfah ﷺ were sitting in the same gathering when someone from the congregation asked a question. Imām Aʿmash ﷺ did not have an answer to this question. However, Imām Abū Ḥanīfah ﷺ, a student of Imām Aʿmash ﷺ, answered the question. Imām Aʿmash ﷺ asked Imām Abū Ḥanīfah ﷺ: "From which evidence did you acquire this answer?" Imām Abū Ḥanīfah ﷺ replied: "From the same ḥadīth which I narrated from you." On hearing this, Imām Aʿmash ﷺ commended the acumen of Imām Abū Ḥanīfah ﷺ, saying:

نَحْنُ الصَّيَادِلَةُ وَأَنْتُمُ الْأَطِبَّاءُ.

We (*muḥaddithūn*) are the dispensers and you are the doctors.[18]

The lessons of Imām Abū Ḥanīfah ﷺ were based upon the Qur'ān and Sunnah.

The erudite Imām Ṣadr al-a'immah al-Makkī ﷺ said:

كَانَ أَبُوْ حَنِيْفَةَ ﷺ يَرْوِيْ أَرْبَعَةَ آلَافِ حَدِيْثٍ: أَلْفَيْنِ لِحَمَّادٍ وَأَلْفَيْنِ لِسَائِرِ الْمَشْيَخَةِ.

18 *Jāmiʿ Bayān al-ʿIlm wa Faḍlihī*, 2:130-131.

> Imām Abū Ḥanīfah ﵀ narrated four thousand ḥadīths: two thousand from Imām Ḥammād ﵀ and two thousand from other shaykhs.[19]

Imām Shams al-Dīn al-Dhahabī ﵀ has included the biography of Imām Abū Ḥanīfah ﵀ in his famous book, *Tadhkirat al-Ḥuffāẓ*, and regarded him amongst the experts of ḥadīth, due to his proficient knowledge in this field.

Imām al-Dhahabī ﵀ began the biographical entry of Imām Abū Ḥanīfah ﵀ with the following titles: the Greatest Imām (*al-Imām al-Aʿẓam*) and the Jurist of Iraq (*Faqīh al-ʿIrāq*). He further writes:

وَكَانَ إِمَامًا، وَرِعًا، عَالِمًا، عَامِلاً، مُتَعَبِّدًا، كَبِيْرَ الشَّانِ، لَا يَقْبَلُ جَوَائِزَ السُّلْطَانِ بَلْ يَتَّجِرُ وَيَكْتَسِبُ.

> He was an imām, pious, a scholar who acted upon his knowledge, and a worshipper. He was a man of high status who would not accept gifts from the ruler, but rather he would trade and earn his own living.[20]

After quoting the aforementioned statement, Mawlānā Ibrāhīm Siyālkawtī* said: "Pure is Allah! In such concise words, he has brilliantly given us the entire picture of his pure life. He did not leave out any vital aspect of his life, with respect to his knowledge, practicing upon it, his general acceptance, self-sufficiency, and his disassociation from rulers and kings."[21]

In addition to this, the erudite imām, Shams al-Dīn Muḥammad ibn Aḥmad al-Maqdisī al-Ḥanbalī ﵀ in his famous book *al-Mukhtaṣar Fī Ṭabaqāt ʿUlamā al-ḥadīth*,[22] and Jalāl al-Dīn

19 *Manāqib Abī Ḥanīfah*, al-Makkī, p. 85.

20 *Tadhkirat al-Ḥuffāẓ*, 1:126.

21 *Tārīkh Ahl-i-Ḥadīth*, p. 79-80.

22 1:270.

al-Suyūṭī ﵀ (d. 911 AH) in *Ṭabaqāt al-Ḥuffāẓ*[23] have mentioned him with immense praise and regarded him amongst the ḥadīth masters (*ḥuffāẓ*).

The testimonies of these great imāms of ḥadīth are evidence of the high status and deep knowledge of Imām Abū Ḥanīfah ﵀. It was due to this reason that students from across the world would come to study by him. It is impossible to count the number of his students, which include Tābi'ūn, ḥadīth scholars (*muḥaddithūn*) and jurists (*fuqahā'*) ﵏. Amongst the four great imāms, Imām Mālik ﵀ was a direct student of Imām Abū Ḥanīfah ﵀, whilst the other two great imāms, Imām Muḥammad ibn Idrīs al-Shāfiʿī ﵀ and Imām Aḥmad ibn Ḥanbal ﵀, and the compilers of the six authentic books of ḥadīth (*ṣiḥāh sittah*), were all students of the students of Imām Abū Ḥanīfah ﵀. Twenty-seven of Imām al-Bukhārī's ﵀ teachers were Imām Abū Ḥanīfah's ﵀ students. Sixty-four reputable narrators of ḥadīth, whose justice and authenticity the imāms of criticism (*jarḥ*) and authentication (*taʿdīl*) have agreed upon, are linked in knowledge with Imām Abū Ḥanīfah ﵀.

The pride of Imām al-Bukhārī's ﵀ *Ṣaḥīh* is the *thulāthiyāt*, i.e., the narrations in whose chains there are only three narrators from Imām Bukhārī ﵀ to Rasūlullāh ﷺ, and they are truly a great honour and source of pride. In *Ṣaḥīh al-Bukhārī*, there are twenty two *thulāthiyāt* in total. Twenty of them are narrated from Imām Abū Ḥanīfa's ﵀ close students and his followers: Imām Makkī ibn Ibrāhīm ﵀, Imām Abū ʿAṣim al- Nabīl ﵀ and Imām Muḥammad ibn ʿAbdullāh al-Anṣārī ﵀.

Allāh Most High illuminated Imām Abū Ḥanīfah's ﵀ academic excellence, like the sun in the sky. There is hardly any Islamic science, be it ḥadīth, jurisprudence (*fiqh*) or Qur'ānic exegesis (*tafsīr*), which has not benefited from him. The Ummah has given him the title of imām due to this immense favour of

23 p. 80.

his. Just as a father makes arrangements for all the necessities of his children, so they can live with comfort and ease in the future, Imām Abū Ḥanīfah derived and systematically compiled juristic rulings to fulfil the needs of the Ummah with respect to living their daily life. May Allāh Most High reward him with the best reward He grants the good-doers. *Āmīn.*

Some non-muqallids claim that his daughter's name was Ḥanīfah, from whom he would ask questions, and this is why he was given the title Abū Ḥanīfah, i.e., the father of Ḥanīfah. There is no cure for such prejuidice from those who claim to follow the ḥadīth, whilst their actions illustrate otherwise. The mouths of such fanatics should be filled with dust. The fact is that the title Abū Ḥanīfah is not a name he chose for himself, but rather a honorary titled conferred to him by the Ummah. Ḥāfiẓ Ibn Ḥajar al-Makkī has mentioned that Imām Abū Ḥanīfah did not have a daughter named Ḥanīfah, on account of whom he was known as Abū Ḥanīfah.[24]

The entire ummah acknowledges Imām Abū Ḥanīfah's academic services and praises his great favour upon the Ummah. The narrator of the first ḥadīth of *Ṣaḥīḥ al-Bukhārī*, Imām Sufyān ibn ʿUyaynah, said:

أَوَّلُ مَنْ صَيَّرَنِي مُحَدِّثًا أَبُوْ حَنِيْفَةَ.

The first person to make me a ḥadīth scholar (*muḥaddith*) was Abū Ḥanīfah.[25]

Imām Abū Dāwūd said:

رَحِمَ اللهُ أَبَا حَنِيْفَةَ، كَانَ إِمَامًا.

May Allah have mercy upon Abū Ḥanīfah. He was an imām.[26]

---

24 *Al-Khayrāt al-Ḥisān*, p.45.

25 *Al-Jawāhir al-Muḍī'ah*, 1:250.

26 *Jāmiʿ Bayān al-ʿIlm wa Faḍlihī*, 2:163.

Imām Yazīd ibn Hārūn ﷺ said: "I met one thousand teachers, and I have taken ḥadīth from most of them. I did not see among them anyone more prudent, more pious and more knowledgable than five of them, the first of them being Abū Ḥanīfah ﷺ."[27]

Imām Shāfiʿī ﷺ deemed all the jurists to be dependant on Imām Abū Ḥanīfah ﷺ.[28]

Mawlānā ʿAbd al-Raḥmān Mubārakpūrī* ﷺ clearly stated that amongst the great scholars of ḥadīth who declared Imām Abū Ḥanīfah ﷺ reliable in ḥadīth are: Imām Yaḥyā ibn Maʿīn ﷺ, Imām ʿAlī ibn al-Madīnī ﷺ, Imām Shuʿbah ﷺ and Imām Sufyān al-Thawrī ﷺ.[29]

Imām Abū Ḥanīfah ﷺ utilised every moment of his life for the service of knowledge and living a life of righteousness. He lived his entire life on the earnings he made from his personal business. He helped the poor and students, and he refused to accept any government post. The Abbasid leader, Manṣūr, offered the post of chief-justice to Imām Abū Ḥanīfah ﷺ, but he refused due to some of the impermissible actions of the government. Being vocal against this injustice led to Imām Abū Ḥanīfah ﷺ being imprisoned. When his fame and acceptance amongst the people increased after imprisonment, Manṣūr had him poisoned.

His martyrdom in the path of Allāh was destined. When he realised that he was poisoned, he fell into prostration and passed away. To Allāh we belong and to Him is our return.

He was martyred in 150 AH (767 AD) and was buried in Baghdad, a centre of Islamic learning. The people of Baghdad reported that they had never before witnessed such a

---

27 *Al-Jawāhir al-Muḍī'ah*, 1:29.

28 *Tārīkh Baghdād*, 13:435.

29 *Taḥqīq al-Kalām*, 2:145.

large funeral, and that no person in the future will be fortunate to witness such a funeral.

The ḥadīth scholars (*muḥaddithūn*) considered the prophecy in the ḥadīth referring to the sons of Persia to be referring to Imām Abū Ḥanīfah, because of his immense service for the religion and his lofty status in knowledge.

It is reported from Sayyidunā Abū Hurayrah that on one occasion, Rasūlullāh placed his blessed hand on Sayyidunā Salmān al-Fārisī and said, "If faith was by the Pleiades (*thurayyā*) star, a man (or he said men) from these people (i.e., the Persians, as Salmān al-Fārisī was Persian) will attain it."[30]

Imām Ḥāfiẓ Muḥammad ibn Yūsuf al-Ṣāliḥī al-Shāfiʿī (d. 942 AH), a famous student of Imām al-Suyūṭī (d. 911 AH), said: "Our Shaykh (Imām al-Suyūṭī) said, with full conviction, that this ḥadīth is referring to Imām Abū Ḥanīfah. There is no doubt in this, because from people of Persian descent, nobody reached the status of Imām Abū Ḥanīfah and his students in knowledge.[31]

Shāh Waliyyullāh al-Muḥaddith al-Dihlawī (d. 1176 AH) and Nawāb Ṣiddiq Ḥasan Khān* (d. 1307 AH) also regarded this ḥadīth to be referring to Imām Abū Ḥanīfah.[32]

30 *Bukhārī* (4897).

31 *ʿUqūd al-Jumān*, p. 45.

32 *Kalimāt Ṭayyibāt*, p. 168; *Itḥāf al-Nubalā'*, p. 45, 424.

Imām al-Dhahabī ﵀ said:
"Leadership in *fiqh* and its intricacies is accepted for this Imām. This is an undoubted matter."

Siyar A'lām al-Nubalā'

INTRODUCTION TO ḤANAFĪ FIQH

Imām Abū Ḥanīfah ﷺ was an imām from the golden era of the Tābiʿūn generation. This era was not a time of conflict and dispute, but rather the Ummah was living in love and harmony due to the blessings of their sincerity and piety. Those without knowledge would trust the scholars, and the scholars were fulfilling their responsibility of guiding people. This was a time when Kufa was the greatest centre of Islamic knowledge, and where Imām Abū Ḥanīfah ﷺ sat at its foremost seat of learning. When Imām Abū Ḥanīfah ﷺ realised that delicate issues will arise in the future, he began to compile juristic rulings from the Qur'ān, Sunnah and the narrations of the Ṣaḥābah ﷺ.

Imām Ṣadr al-a'immah Muwaffaq al-Makkī ﷺ said:

وأَبُوْ حَنِيْفَةَ أَوَّلُ مَنْ دَوَّنَ عِلْمَ هَذِهِ الشَّرِيْعَةِ، لَمْ يَسْبِقْهُ أَحَدٌ مِمَّنْ قَبْلَهُ.

Abū Ḥanīfah was the first person to compile the knowledge of the sacred law (*sharīʿah*). Nobody preceded him in this regard.[33]

Imām al-Suyūṭī al-Shāfiʿī ﷺ has written under the discussion of the special qualities of Imām Abū Ḥanīfah ﷺ:

أَنَّهُ أَوَّلُ مَنْ دَوَّنَ عِلْمَ الشَّرِيْعَةِ وَرَتَّبَهَا أَبْوَابًا، ثُمَّ تَبِعَهُ مَالِكُ بْنُ أَنَسٍ ﷺ فِي تَرْتِيْبِ الْمُوَطَّأِ، وَلَمْ يَسْبِقْ أَبَا حَنِيْفَةَ ﷺ أَحَدٌ، لِأَنَّ الصَّحَابَةَ وَالتَّابِعِيْنَ لَمْ

33 *Manāqib Abī Ḥanīfah*, Muwaffaq al-Makkī, 2:136.

يَضَعُوْا فِيْ عُلُوْمِ الشَّرِيْعَةِ أَبْوَابًا مُبَوَّبَةً وَلَا كُتُبًا مُرَتَّبَةً، وَإِنَّمَا كَانُوْا يَعْتَمِدُوْنَ عَلَى قُوَّةِ حِفْظِهِمْ، فَلَمَّا رَأَى أَبُوْ حَنِيْفَةَ ﷺ الْعِلْمَ مُنْتَشِرًا وَخَافَ عَلَيْهِ الضِّيَاعَ دَوَّنَهُ فَجَعَلَهُ أَبْوَابًا.

He was the first to compile the knowledge of the sacred law (*sharīʿah*) and organise it into chapters. He was then followed by Mālik ibn Anas ﷺ in his compilation of the *Muwaṭṭa'*. Nobody prior to Abū Ḥanīfah ﷺ had done this, as the Ṣaḥābah and Tābiʿūn did not compile the sciences of the sacred law (*sharīʿah*) in separate chapters or arranged books. They only relied on the strength of their memory. However, when Abū Ḥanīfah ﷺ saw that knowledge was scattered and he feared it may be lost, he compiled it into chapters.[34]

Imām Ibn Ḥajar al-Makkī ﷺ states under the discussion of the special qualities of Imām Abū Ḥanīfah ﷺ:

أَنَّهُ أَوَّلُ مَنْ دَوَّنَ عِلْمَ الْفِقْهِ وَرَتَّبَهُ أَبْوَابًا، وَكَتَبَ عَلَى نَحْوِ مَا هُوَ عَلَيْهِ، وَ تَبِعَهُ مَالِكٌ فِيْ مُوَطَّئِهِ، وَمَنْ قَبْلَهُ إِنَّمَا كَانُوْا يَعْتَمِدُوْنَ عَلَى حِفْظِهِمْ، وَهُوَ أَوَّلُ مَنْ وَضَعَ كِتَابَ الْفَرَائِضِ وَكِتَابَ الشُّرُوْطِ.

He was the first person to compile the science of jurisprudence (*fiqh*) and organise it into chapters. He wrote it in the manner it is today. Mālik ibn Anas ﷺ followed him in his Muwaṭṭa'. Those before him would rely on their memory. He was also the first person to compile the book of inheritance (*farā'iḍ*) and conditions (*shurūṭ*).[35]

Imāṃ Abū Ḥanīfah ﷺ selected, from amongst his thousands of students, forty reputable scholars who were imāms of the

34 *Tabyīḍ al-Ṣaḥīfah*, p. 36.
35 *Al-Khayrāt al-Ḥisān*, p. 28.

time, to help him in the compilation and giving sequence to his jurisprudence (*fiqh*).

Imām al-Ṭāḥāwī ﷺ (d. 321 AH) reported with a connected chain from Imām Asad ibn al-Furāt ﷺ (d. 213 AH):

كَانَ أَصْحَابُ أَبِيْ حَنِيْفَةَ ﷺ الَّذِيْنَ دَوَّنُوا الْكُتُبَ أَرْبَعِيْنَ رَجُلًا، فَكَانَ فِي الْعَشَرَةِ الْمُتَقَدِّمِيْنَ أَبُوْ يُوْسُفَ وَ زُفَرُ وَدَاوُدُ الطَّائِيُّ وَأَسَدُ بْنُ عَمْرٍو وَيُوْسُفُ بْنُ خَالِدِ السَّمْتِيُّ وَ يَحْيَى بْنُ زَكَرِيَّا بْنِ أَبِيْ زَائِدَةَ، وَهُوَ الَّذِيْ كَانَ يَكْتُبُهَا لَهُمْ ثَلَاثِيْنَ سَنَةً.

The students of Abū Ḥanīfah ﷺ who compiled (his rulings) into books were forty. Amongst the ten senior students were Abū Yūsuf, Zufar, Dāwūd al-Ṭā'ī, Asad ibn ʿAmr, Yūsuf ibn Khālid al-Samtī (Imām al-Shāfiʿī's teacher) and Yaḥyā ibn Zakariyyā ibn Abī Zā'idah, who used to write (i.e., the juristic rulings) for them for thirty years."[36]

Once, a person said to the great ḥadīth scholar (*muḥaddith*), Imām Wakīʿ ibn al-Jarrāḥ ﷺ (d. 197 AH), that Imām Abū Ḥanīfah ﷺ erred in a certain issue. Upon this, Imām Wakīʿ ﷺ repr - manded that person by saying:

كَيْفَ يَقْدِرُ أَبُوْ حَنِيْفَةَ ﷺ يُخْطِئُ وَمَعَهُ مِثْلُ أَبِيْ يُوْسُفَ وَزُفَرَ فِى قِيَاسِهِمَا، وَمِثْلُ يَحْيَى بْنِ أَبِيْ زَائِدَةَ وَحَفْصِ بْنِ غِيَاثٍ وَحِبَّانَ وَمُنْدَلٍ فِيْ حِفْظِهِمُ الْحَدِيْثَ، وَالْقَاسِمِ بْنِ مَعْنٍ فِيْ مَعْرِفَتِهِ بِاللُّغَةِ الْعَرَبِيَّةِ، وَدَاوُدَ الطَّائِيِّ وَفُضَيْلِ بْنِ عِيَاضٍ فِيْ زُهْدِهِمَا وَ وَرَعِهِمَا؟ مَنْ كَانَ هٰؤُلَاءِ جُلَسَاؤُهُ لَمْ يَكَدْ يُخْطِئُ، لِأَنَّهُ إِنْ أَخْطَأَ رَدُّوْهُ.

How can Abū Ḥanīfah err, when he has with him the likes of Abū Yūsuf and Zufar in analogy (*qiyās*); the likes

36 *Al-Jawāhir al-Muḍī'ah*, 2:211-212.

> of Yaḥyā ibn Abī Zā'idah, Ḥafs ibn Ghiyāth and Mundal in their memorisation of ḥadīth; Qāsim ibn Maʿn in his knowledge of Arabic; and Dāwūd al-Ṭā'ī and Fuḍayl ibn ʿIyāḍ in their abstinence and piety? One who has such people as his companions is not likely to err, because they will correct him if he does.[37]

Imām Ṣadr al-A'immah ﵀ explained the consultative manner in which the Ḥanafī school was formed:

> فَوَضَعَ أَبُوْ حَنِيْفَةَ ﵀ مَذْهَبَهُ شُوْرَى بَيْنَهُمْ لَمْ يَسْتَبِدَّ فِيْهِ بِنَفْسِهِ دُوْنَهُمْ، اجْتِهَادًا مِنْهُ فِي الدِّيْنِ وَمُبَالَغَةً فِي النَصِيْحَةِ لِلهِ وَرَسُوْلِهِ وَالْمُؤْمِنِيْنَ، فَكَانَ يُلْقِي الْمَسَائِلَ مَسْئَلَةً مَسْئَلَةً، وَيَسْمَعُ مَا عِنْدَهُمْ وَيَقُوْلُ مَا عِنْدَهُ، وَيُنَاظِرُهُمْ شَهْرًا أَوْ أَكْثَرَ مِنْ ذَلِكَ، حَتَّى يَسْتَقِرَّ أَحَدُ الْأَقْوَالِ فِيْهَا، ثُمَّ يُثْبِتُهَا أَبُوْ يُوْسُفَ ﵀ فِي الْأُصُوْلِ حَتَّى أَثْبَتَ الْأُصُوْلَ كُلَّهَا.

> Imām Abū Ḥanīfah formed his school through mutual consultation. He did not do things independently without them. He did this out of striving for the religion, and being sincere to Allah, His Rasūl ﷺ and the believers. He would present rulings one at a time. He would listen to their views, state his own opinions, and discuss with them for as long as a month or more, until one opinion therein was decided. Abū Yūsuf would then write this in the main rulings, until he had compiled them all.[38]

One can imagine how much effort and research was put into compiling the Ḥanafī school. The great imām in ḥadīth sciences, Imām ʿAbdullāh ibn al-Mubārak ﵀ said regarding the research behind just one issue:

---

37 *Tarīkh Baghdād*, 14:250.

38 *Manāqib Abī Ḥanīfah*, by Muwaffaq al-Makkī, 2:133.

فَخَاضُوْا فِيْهَا ثَلَاثَةَ أَيَّامٍ بِالْغَدَاةِ وَالْعَشِيِّ.

They (i.e., the members of the consultative board) delved into it for three days, from morning till evening.[39]

After years of effort and research by the scholars in this consultative board, under the guidance of Imām Abū Ḥanīfah ﷺ, the rulings of the Ḥanafī school of jurisprudence (*fiqh*) were formed.

Mullā ʿAlī al-Qārī ﷺ said:

أَنَّهُ وَضَعَ ثَلَاثَةً وَثَمَانِيْنَ أَلْفَ مَسْئَلَةً، مِنْهَا ثَمَانِيَةٌ وَثَلَاثُوْنَ أَلْفًا فِي الْعِبَادَةِ، وَالْبَاقِيْ فِي الْمُعَامَلَاتِ.

He compiled eighty-three thousand issues: thirty-eight thousand of them were regarding worship, and the remainder were regarding dealings.[40]

The likes of Imām Abū Yūsuf ﷺ, and other erudite jurists, were responsible for compiling the Ḥanafī fiqh. Imām Muḥammad ibn al-Ḥasan ﷺ also compiled rulings of the Ḥanafī school in his works, and which reached the Ummah through uninterrupted succession to this day. According to the methodology at the time, the rulings of the Ḥanafī school were compiled in various books, in the form of narrations.

These books of Imām Muḥammad ibn al-Ḥasan are known as *ẓāhir al-riwāyah*, which include six of his works: *al-Mabsūṭ*, *al-Ziyādāt*, *al-Siyar al-Ṣaghīr*, *al-Siyar al-Kabīr*, *al-Jāmiʿ al-Ṣaghīr* and *al-Jāmiʿ al-Kabīr*. The fiqh that was compiled under the supervision of Imām Abū Ḥanīfah is the same *ẓāhir al-riwāyah*, which was documented in light of Qur'ānic verses, ḥadīths and narrations (*āthār*) [i.e., from the Ṣaḥābah ﷺ]. At the time, most issues

39 *Manāqib Abī Ḥanīfah*, by Muwaffaq al-Makkī, 2:54.

40 *Dhayl al-Jawāhir*, 2:472.

were written with their evidence and source. However, for the benefit of the general masses, these issues were compiled in books like *Mukhtaṣar al-Qudūrī*, *Kanz al-Daqā'iq*, and so forth.

It is clear from this brief introduction that the Ḥanafī fiqh is not foreign to the Qur'ān and Sunnah; in fact, it is derived from the Qur'ān and Sunnah, and its issues are connected back to their evidences. It is for this reason that Allāh Most High granted acceptance to the Ḥanafī fiqh throughout the world.

The famous historian, Imām Ibn Khaldūn ؒ (d. 808 AH), said: "As for Abū Ḥanīfah, today the people of Iraq, the Muslims of India [i.e, the Indian Subcontinent], China, Transoxiana, and all of the non-Arab lands follow him."[41]

If any sapling of today labels the Ḥanafī fiqh, which was compiled in the era of the Tābiʿūn, the best of eras (*khayr al-qurūn*) as stated in ḥadīths, to be in opposition to the Qur'ān and Sunnah, this opponent to the practice of the whole Ummah will be reminded of the words of Imām Abū Ḥanīfah ؒ:

إِنْ يَّحْسُدُوْنِي فَإِنِّيْ غَيْرُ لَائِمِهِمْ
قَبْلِيْ مِنَ النَّاسِ اَهْلُ الْفَضْلِ قَدْ حُسِدُوْا
فَدَامَ لِيْ وَلَهُمْ مَابِيْ وَمَابِهِمْ
وَمَاتَ اَكْثَرُنَا غَيْظًا بِمَا يَجِدُ

If they are jealous of me, I will not rebuke them;
People of virtue before me have been envied.
May my situation remain the same for me, and their situation remain the same for them;
And may the one whose heart is most enraged die due to the rage he feels.[42]

---

41 *Muqaddamah Ibn Khaldūn*, p. 445.

42 *Tārīkh Baghdād*, 15:502.

The famous Imām and grammarian, Maḥmūd al-Zamakhsharī, said in praise of Imām Abū Ḥanīfah:

وَتَدَ اللهُ تَعَالَى الْأَرْضَ بِالْأَعْلَامِ الْمَنِيْفَةِ،

كَمَا وَتَدَ الْحَنِيْفِيَّةَ بِعُلُوْمِ أَبِيْ حَنِيْفَةَ.

Allah Most High strengthened the earth with firm mountains, like He strengthened the monotheistic way (*ḥanīfiyyah*) with the knowledge of Abū Ḥanīfah.[43]

43 *Al-Rawḍ al-Bāsim fī 'l-Dhabb 'an Sunnat Abī 'l-Qāsim*, 1:311.

The Prophet ﷺ said:
"Whoever memorises forty ḥadīths regarding matters of the religion for my Ummah, Allāh ﷻ will resurrect him as a jurist, and I will be an intercessor and witness for him on the Day of Judgement."

Sharaf Aṣḥāb al-Ḥadīth

Ḥadīth 1
ṢALĀH TIMINGS

Allāh ﷻ made five daily ṣalāhs obligatory upon every sane, mature Muslim. To perform these five daily ṣalāhs at their fixed times is imperative.

Allāh ﷻ said:

إِنَّ ٱلصَّلَوٰةَ كَانَتْ عَلَى الْمُؤْمِنِيْنَ كِتٰبًا مَّوْقُوْتًا

Indeed, ṣalāh is an obligation on the believers that is fixed with time.[44]

Sayyidunā ʿAbdullāh ibn ʿAmr ibn al-ʿĀṣ ؓ narrated that Rasūlullāh ﷺ elaborated the timings of the five ṣalāhs as follows:

وَقْتُ الظُّهْرِ إِذَا زَالَتِ الشَّمْسُ وَكَانَ ظِلُّ الرَّجُلِ كَطُوْلِهِ مَا لَمْ تَحْضُرِ الْعَصْرُ، وَوَقْتُ الْعَصْرِ مَا لَمْ تَصْفَرَّ الشَّمْسُ، وَوَقْتُ صَلٰوةِ الْمَغْرِبِ مَالَمْ يَغِبِ الشَّفَقُ، وَوَقْتُ صَلٰوةِ الْعِشَاءِ إِلَى نِصْفِ اللَّيْلِ الْأَوْسَطِ، وَوَقْتُ صَلٰوةِ الْصُّبْحِ مِنْ طُلُوْعِ الْفَجْرِ مَا لَمْ تَطْلُعِ الشَّمْسُ.

The time for ẓuhr ṣalāh is when the sun moves (past the meridian) and a man's shadow is equal to his height, as long as the time for ʿaṣr ṣalāh does not come. The time for ʿaṣr ṣalāh is as long as the sun does not become pale (the time after the sun becomes pale until maghrib is the disliked (*makrūh*) time for ʿaṣr). The time for maghrib ṣalāh

44 Qur'ān, 4:103.

> is (from sunset) as long as the twilight (*shafaq*) does not disappear. The time for ʿishā' ṣalāh is until the middle of the night. The time for fajr ṣalāh is from the appearance of dawn, as long as the sun has not risen.[45]

Three points in the abovementioned ḥadīth require clarification:

1. The ending time of maghrib is the disappearance of the twilight (*shafaq*). According to Imām Abū Ḥanīfah, *shafaq* is the whiteness that appears at night on the horizon after the redness disappears, whereafter it becomes totally dark, as will be explained later under ḥadīth five.

2. This hadith states the ending time for ʿishā' to be the middle of the night. However, some narrations mention one third of the night, and in other narrations, the appearance of dawn has also been mentioned. The jurists (*fuqahā'*) reconciled between these different narrations and decided that the best time to perform ʿishā' is until the first third of the night, performing it until the middle of the night is less virtuous, and to delay it until the appearance of dawn is reprehensible (*makrūh*).[46]

   Imām Amīr al-Ṣanʿānī* (d. 1183 AH) and ʿAllāmah al-Shawkānī* (d. 1255 AH) both hold a similar position.[47]

3. It is clear from the aforementioned Qur'ānic verse and ḥadīth that the time for each ṣalāh is fixed, and it is compulsory to perform each ṣalāh at its fixed time. Therefore, it is impermissible to combine two ṣalāhs at one time. However, in the ḥajj pilgrimage, on the ninth of Dhū 'l-Ḥijjah, it is valid to combine ẓuhr and ʿaṣr ṣalāhs at the time of ẓuhr in ʿArafāt

45 *Muslim* (1387).

46 *Sharḥ Maʿānī al-Āthār*, 1:109; *Āthār al-Sunan*, p. 95.

47 *Nayl al-Awṭār*, 1:242; *Subul al-Salām*, 1:111.

(behind the imām of Masjid Namirah), and on the same day, it is necessary to combine maghrib and ʿishā' ṣalāhs in ʿishā' time in Muzdalifah, as stated by Sayyidunā ʿAbdullāh ibn Masʿūd ﷺ:

كَانَ رَسُوْلُ اللهِ ﷺ يُصَلِّي الصَّلٰوةَ لِوَقْتِهَا إِلا بِجَمْعٍ وَعَرَفَاتٍ.

The Prophet ﷺ used to perform (every) ṣalāh at its fixed time, except in Jamʿ (Muzdalifah) and ʿArafāt.[48]

Apart from these two scenarios, it is not permissible to combine two ṣalāhs under any circumstance. As for those ḥadīths - apart from the ḥadīth of ʿArafāt and Muzdalifah - which mention combining two ṣalāhs, they mean apparent combining (*jamʿ ṣūrī*), not real combining (*jamʿ ḥaqīqī*). The meaning of apparent combining is to perform ẓuhr ṣalāh at its end time and ʿaṣr ṣalāh at its beginning time.

Similarly, maghrib ṣalāh is performed at its end time and ʿishā' ṣalāh at its beginning time. In this manner, there will be an apparent combination (*jamʿ ṣūrī*) of two ṣalāhs, but not an actual combination (*jamʿ ḥaqīqī*). Sayyidunā ʿAbdullāh ibn ʿAbbās, Sayyidunā ʿAbdullāh ibn ʿUmar and others ﷺ (who are also narrators of the ḥadīths on combining) have all narrated the same method.[49]

ʿAllāmah al-Shawkānī, Nawāb Ṣiddīq Ḥasan Khān*, Nawāb Nūr al-Ḥasan*, and other non-muqallid scholars, have given preference to apparent combining, and they have clearly said it is important that the narrations of combining ṣalāhs be interpreted as apparent combining, because the Ṣaḥābah ﷺ who narrated these narrations interpreted it as such.[50]

48 *Bukhārī* (1682); *Muslim* (3094); *Nasā'ī* (3012).

49 *Nasā'ī* (591, 597).

50 *Nayl al-Awṭār*, 1:629; *Dalīl al-Ṭālib*, p. 348, *ʿArf al-Jādī*, p. 19.

Ḥadīth 2
THE END TIME FOR ẒUHR ṢALĀH AND BEGINNING TIME OF ʿAṢR ṢALĀH

The scholars differ regarding the ending time of ẓuhr and beginning time of ʿaṣr. According to Imām Abū Ḥanīfah ﵀ (d. 150 AH), the time of ẓuhr is until two *mithls*, i.e., when the shadow of everything becomes twice its size (excluding its original shadow at the meridian), and after that, the time for ʿaṣr begins.

Imām Abū Ḥanīfah's evidence is the following ḥadīth, which has been reported by Sayyidunā ʿAbdullāh ibn ʿUmar ﵄ that Rasūlullāh ﷺ said:

إِنَّمَا أَجَلُكُمْ فِيْ أَجَلِ مَنْ خَلَا مِنَ الْأُمَمِ مَا بَيْنَ صَلٰوةِ العَصْرِ إِلىٰ مَغْرِبِ الشَّمْسِ، وَإِنَّمَا مَثَلُكُمْ وَمَثَلُ الْيَهُوْدِ وَالنَّصَارٰى كَرَجُلٍ اسْتَعْمَلَ عُمَّالًا، فَقَالَ: مَنْ يَّعْمَلُ لِيْ إِلىٰ نِصْفِ النَّهَارِ عَلَى قِيْرَاطٍ قِيْرَاطٍ؟ فَعَمِلَتِ الْيَهُوْدُ إِلٰى نِصْفِ النَّهَارِ عَلَى قِيْرَاطٍ قِيْرَاطٍ، ثُمَّ قَالَ: مَنْ يَّعْمَلُ لِيْ مِنْ نِصْفِ النَّهَارِ إِلَى صَلٰوةِ الْعَصْرِ عَلَى قِيْرَاطٍ قِيْرَاطٍ؟ فَعَمِلَتِ النَّصَارٰى مِنْ نِصْفِ النَّهَارِ إِلَى صَلٰوةِ الْعَصْرِ عَلَى قِيْرَاطٍ قِيْرَاطٍ، ثُمَّ قَالَ: مَنْ يَّعْمَلُ لِيْ مِنْ صَلٰوةِ الْعَصْرِ إِلَى مَغْرِبِ الشَّمْسِ عَلَى قِيْرَاطَيْنِ قِيْرَاطَيْنِ؟ أَلَا فَأَنْتُمُ الَّذِيْنَ يَعْمَلُوْنَ مِنْ صَلٰوةِ الْعَصْرِ إِلَى مَغْرِبِ الشَّمْسِ عَلَى قِيْرَاطَيْنِ قِيْرَاطَيْنِ، أَلَا لَكُمُ الْأَجْرُ مَرَّتَيْنِ. فَغَضِبَ الْيَهُوْدُ وَالنَّصَارٰى، فَقَالُوْا: نَحْنُ أَكْثَرُ عَمَلًا وَأَقَلُّ عَطَاءً، قَالَ اللهُ: وَهَلْ ظَلَمْتُكُمْ مِنْ حَقِّكُمْ شَيْأً؟ قَالُوْا لَا، قَالَ اللهُ: فَإِنَّهُ فَضْلِيْ، أُعْطِيْهِ مَنْ شِئْتُ.

Your lifespan, in comparison to the lifespan of past nations, is like the period between ʿaṣr ṣalāh and sunset. Your similitude and the similitude of the Jews and Christians is that of a person who employed labourers and said to them, "Who will work for me till midday for one carat each?" The Jews then worked until midday for one carat each. He then said: "Who will work for me from midday till ʿaṣr ṣalāh for one carat each?" The Christians then worked from midday until ʿaṣr ṣalāh for one carat each. He then asked, "Who will work for me from ʿaṣr ṣalāh until sunset for two carats each?" Surely, it is you who are working from ʿaṣr ṣalāh till maghrib ṣalāh for two carats each; for you is double reward. The Jews and the Christians became angry, saying, "We did more work but took less wages." He said: "Have I at all wronged you in your due?" They replied, "No". He said, "This is My extra grace; I grant it to whom I wish (i.e., giving more reward to the Muslims, despite their work being less)."[51]

The evidence for ẓuhr time ending upon two *mithls* is deduced from the aforementioned ḥadīth, as follows: The Prophet ﷺ deemed the duration of the work of the Muslims (from ʿaṣr to maghrib) to be less than the duration of the work of the Christians (from ẓuhr until ʿaṣr). This can only be if the end time for ẓuhr is two *mithls*, because if ẓuhr time ended upon only one *mithl*, the duration between ẓuhr and ʿaṣr will be less than the duration between ʿaṣr and maghrib, leaving no conformity in the similitude.[52]

This position is also supported by a ḥadīth that has a strong chain on the authority of Sayyidunā Jābir ؓ: "One day, Rasūlullāh ﷺ lead us in ẓuhr ṣalāh after the first *mithl*, and he lead us in ʿaṣr ṣalāh after the second *mithl*."[53]

This position is further strengthened by the narration of

51 *Bukhārī* (557).

52 *ʿUmdat al-Qārī*, 1:352; *Irshād al-Sārī*, 2:32.

53 *Muṣannaf Ibn Abī Shaybah*, 1:353; *ʿUmdat al-Qārī*, 5:49.

Sayyidunā Abū Hurayrah ؓ in which he commanded his own student about the timings of ṣalāh. He said to him:

صَلِّ الظُّهْرَ إِذَا كَانَ ظِلُّكَ مِثْلَكَ، وَالْعَصْرَ إِذَا كَانَ ظِلُّكَ مِثْلَيْكَ.

Perform ẓuhr ṣalāh when the length of your shadow is equal to you (one *mithl*), and perform ʿaṣr ṣalāh when the length of your shadow is twice your size (two *mithls*).[54]

In this narration, Sayyidunā Abū Hurayrah ؓ instructed his student to perform ẓuhr after one *mithl*, and ʿaṣr after two *mithls*. This is evidence to the fact that the time for ẓuhr remains after one *mithl*, and the time for ʿaṣr does not begin after one *mithl*, but rather starts after two *mithls*. Some people interpreted this narration as referring to the end time of ẓuhr and ʿaṣr, but this interpretation is incorrect, because this will necessitate the time for ʿaṣr ṣalāh ending on two *mithls*. An authentic ḥadīth narrated on the authority of Sayyidunā Abū Hurayrah ؓ himself states that Rasūlullāh ﷺ said, "Whoever attains one *rakʿah* of ʿaṣr before sunset, he has attained the (time for) ʿaṣr ṣalāh."[55]

Some narrations state the end time for ẓuhr to be one *mithl*. Hence, some scholars have reconciled both ḥadīths by saying one should perform ẓuhr ṣalāh before one *mithl* and ʿaṣr ṣalāh after two *mithls*, thereby acting upon both types of narration.

54 *Muwaṭṭa'* (9).

55 *Muwaṭṭa'* (5). Also see *Subul al-Salām*, 1:111.

Ḥadīth 3
THE *SUNNAH* TIME FOR ẒUHR ṢALĀH

In hot weather, ẓuhr ṣalāh should be delayed until the intensity of the heat reduces, and in cool weather, ẓuhr ṣalāh should be performed without any delay. This was the practice of Rasūlullāh ﷺ. Sayyidunā Anas ibn Mālik ؓ said:

كَانَ رَسُوْلُ اللهِ إِذَا كَانَ الْحَرُّ أَبْرَدَ بِالصَّلٰوةِ، وَإِذَا كَانَ الْبَرْدُ عَجَّلَ.

When it was hot, Rasūlullāh ﷺ would wait until it cooled down to perform ṣalāh, and when it was cold he would hasten.[56]

Shaykh Nāṣir al-Dīn al-Albānī* said this ḥadīth is authentic.[57] In many authentic ḥadīths, Rasūlullāh ﷺ said:

إِذَا اشْتَدَّ الْحَرُّ فَأَبْرِدُوْا عَنِ الصَّلَاةِ، فَإِنَّ شِدَّةَ الْحَرِّ مِنْ فَيْحِ جَهَنَّمَ.

When the heat is intense, perform (ẓuhr) ṣalāh when it becomes cooler, for indeed, the intensity of the heat is from the raging of Hell.[58]

This ruling is equally applicable to travelling and whilst being resident. The purpose of performing ẓuhr ṣalāh when the intensity of the heat reduces is to bring ease for the people that are performing the ṣalāh and to remove any difficulty from them. Going to the masjid to perform ṣalāh in such heat and to attain proper concentration and devotion, which is the spirit of ṣalāh, is difficult. This reasoning applies in both scenarios, i.e., being resident and travelling. Hence, to differentiate between the ruling for a resident person and a traveller, due to one

---

56 *Nasā'ī* (499).
57 *Mishkāt al-Maṣābīḥ*, ed. Nāṣir al-Dīn al-Albānī, 1:195.
58 *Bukhārī* (533-539); *Muslim* (1394-1402).

isolated incident of a journey, in comparison to the general ḥadīths is incorrect.[59]

Imām Bukhārī's ؒ opinion is that there should be no distinction in the ruling of a resident person and a traveller. Hence, in his *Ṣaḥīh*, he first mentioned the general ḥadīths pertaining to performing ẓuhr ṣalāh when the heat reduces, and thereafter he mentioned the ḥadīth in which Rasūlullāh ﷺ instructed the Ṣaḥābah to perform ẓuhr ṣalāh when the heat had reduced whilst they were on a journey. Imām al-Bukhārī gave the following chapter title to the ḥadīth: *Bāb al-ibrād bi 'l-ẓuhr fī 'l-safar* (chapter regarding performing ẓuhr ṣalāh whilst on a journey when the heat reduces).

The ḥadīth commentators, Ḥāfiẓ Badr al-Dīn al-ʿAynī, Ḥāfiẓ Ibn Ḥajar al-ʿAsqalānī, Ḥāfiẓ al-Qasṭalānī and others stated when commenting on the aforementioned chapter-heading that Imām Bukhārī's ؒ indication through this chapter-heading is that performing ẓuhr ṣalāh when the heat reduces is not exclusive to a resident person, but rather the ruling applies to a resident person and a traveller.[60]

Mawlānā Shams al-Ḥaqq Aẓīmābādī* ؒ (d. 1329 AH) has similarly stated that the reason for performing ẓuhr ṣalāh when the heat reduces is to create ease for people.[61] He has also stated the followed principle:

وَقَدْ تَقَرَّرَ أَنَّ وَقَائِعَ الْأَعْيَانِ لَا يُحْتَجُّ بِهَا عَلَى الْعُمُوْمِ.

It is an established fact that specific incidents cannot be evidence for general rulings.[62]

Therefore, it is incorrect for some to deem this ruling exclusive to travelling, by using the ḥadīth in which Rasūlullāh ﷺ

59 *ʿUmdat al-Qārī'*, 5:36-37.

60 Ibid; *Fatḥ al-Bārī*, 2:124, *Irshād al-Sārī*, 2:19.

61 *ʿAwn al-Maʿbūd*, 1:404.

62 *ʿAwn al-Maʿbūd*, 2:428.

gave the instruction to perform ẓuhr ṣalāh when the heat had reduced whilst travelling.

Moreover, Imām Amīr al-Ṣanʿānī (d. 1183 AH), ʿAllāmah al-Shawkānī (d. 1255 AH), ʿAllāmah Waḥīd al-Zamān* (d. 1338 AH), ʿAllāmah Nūr al-Ḥasan (d. 1336 AH), and other non-muqallid scholars clearly said delaying ẓuhr ṣalāh on hot days is better; they did not restrict this to travelling only.[63]

❧

Ḥadīth 4
THE *SUNNAH* TIME FOR ʿAṢR ṢALĀH

It is *sunnah* to slightly delay ʿaṣr ṣalāh, but not to the extent that the sun turns pale (such that a person is able to look directly at the sun), because when the sun turns pale the reprehensible (*makrūh*) time of ʿaṣr begins.

Sayyidunā ʿAlī ibn Shaybān ﷺ said:

قَدِمْنَا عَلَى رَسُوْلِ اللهِ الْمَدِيْنَةَ، فَكَانَ يُؤَخِّرُ الْعَصْرَ مَا دَامَتِ الشَّمْسُ بَيْضَاءَ نَقِيَّةً.

> We came to Rasūlullāh ﷺ in Madīnah. He would delay the ʿaṣr ṣalāh as long as the sun remained bright and clear.[64]

Imām Abū Dāwūd (d. 275 AH), after narrating this ḥadīth in his *Sunan*, remained silent upon it and has not critiqued it. Imām Abū Dāwūd himself stated a principle regarding his narrations: "Whichever ḥadīth I remain silent upon is sound (*ḥasan*)."[65]

---

63 *Subul al-Salām*, 1:114; *Nayl al-Awṭār*, 1:226; *Nuzul al-Abrār*, p. 57; *Fatḥ al-ʿAllām*, p. 11.

64 *Abū Dāwūd* (408).

65 *Al-Bāʿith al-Ḥathīth*, p. 50.

Both ʿAllāmah Muḥammad Aḥmad Shākir* and Mawlānā Badīʿ al-Dīn Rāshidī* accepted this principle.[66]

ʿAllāmah al-Shawkānī (d. 1255 AH) said:

إِنَّ جَمَاعَةً مِنْ أَئِمَّةِ الْحَدِيْثِ صَرَّحُوْا بِصَلَاحِيَّةِ مَا سَكَتَ عَنْهُ أَبُوْ دَاوُدَ لِلْإِحْتِجَاجِ.

A group of imāms of ḥadīth clearly stated that a ḥadīth upon which Abū Dāwūd remains silent is credible as evidence.[67]

Thus, the ḥadīth of Abū Dāwūd is sound and qualifies as evidence, and the objections on some of its narrators are invalid, in light of the accepted principles of non-muqallid scholars themselves. This ḥadīth is further strengthened by many more narrations, such as the ḥadīth reported by Umm al-Mu'minīn Umm Salamah ﵂:

كَانَ رَسُوْلُ اللهِ ﷺ أَشَدَّ تَعْجِيْلًا لِلظُّهْرِ مِنْكُمْ، وَأَنْتُمْ أَشَدُّ تَعْجِيْلًا لِلْعَصْرِ مِنْه.

Rasūlullāh ﷺ would hasten ẓuhr more than you, whilst you hasten ʿaṣr more than him.[68]

Shaykh Nāṣir al-Dīn Albānī deemed this ḥadīth to be authentic.[69] This ḥadīth also proves that Rasūlullāh ﷺ would not perform ʿaṣr in its beginning time, but rather he would delay it. In addition, this position can be supported through the consensus of the scholars that ʿaṣr ṣalāh should be delayed and performed after the second *mithl*.

Shaykh al-Islām Imām Ibn ʿAbd al-Barr al-Mālikī ﵀ said:

---

66 *Al-Bāʿith al-Ḥathīth*, p. 51; *Maqālāt Rāshidiyyah*, 3:492.

67 *Nayl al-Awṭār*, 1:391.

68 *Tirmidhī* (161).

69 *Tirmidhī*, ed. Nāṣir al-Dīn al-Albānī, p. 50.

وَقَدْ أَجْمَعَ الْعُلَمَاءُ عَلَى أَنَّ مَنْ صَلَّى الْعَصْرَ وَالشَّمْسُ بَيْضَاءُ نَقِيَّةٌ لَمْ تَدْخُلْهَا صُفْرَةٌ فَقَدْ صَلَّاهَا فِي وَقْتِهَا الْمُخْتَارِ، وَفِيْ ذَلِكَ دَلِيْلٌ عَلَى أَنَّ مُرَاعَاةَ الْمِثْلَيْنِ عِنْدَهُمْ اِسْتِحْبَابٌ.

The scholars unanimously agreed that whoever performs ʿaṣr ṣalāh, whilst the sun is bright and clear and no paleness has come upon it, he has performed it at its best time. This also contains evidence that taking *two mithls* into consideration is laudable according to them.[70]

Ḥadīth 5
THE END TIME FOR MAGHRIB ṢALĀH AND THE BEGINNING TIME FOR ʿISHĀ ṢALĀH

In ḥadīth one, it has passed that when the twilight (*shafaq*) disappears, the time of maghrib has finished and the time of ʿishā' has started. Twilight, according to Imām Abū Ḥanīfah ﵀, is the whiteness that spreads across the horizon in the evening and appears after the redness disappears.

Imām Abū Ḥanīfah's ﵀ evidence is a lengthy ḥadīth reported by Ṭabarānī[71] from Sayyidunā Jābir ibn ʿAbdullāh ﵁, in which he explains Rasūlullāh's ﷺ timings of ṣalāh:

ثُمَّ أَذَّنَ لِلْعِشَاءِ حِيْنَ ذَهَبَ بَيَاضُ النَّهَارِ، وَهُوَ الشَّفَقُ، ثُمَّ أَمَرَهُ فَأَقَامَ الصَّلَاةَ فَصَلَّى.

Thereafter, Bilāl ﵁ gave *adhān* for ʿishā' ṣalāh when the whiteness of daylight had disappeared, and this is the

70 *Al-Tamhīd*, 3:383.
71 *Al-Muʿjam al-Awsaṭ* (6787).

twilight (*shafaq*). Thereafter, he ﷺ instructed him to perform the *iqāmah*, thus he did so and he ﷺ performed (ʿishā') ṣalāh.

Imām al-Haythamī (d. 807 AH) classified this ḥadīth as authentic.[72] Furthermore, the ḥadīth is supported by other authentic narrations.[73]

❧

Ḥadīth 6
THE *SUNNAH* TIME FOR MAGHRIB ṢALĀH

It is *sunnah* to perform maghrib ṣalāh immediately after sunset, because this was the practice of Rasūlullāh ﷺ.

Sayyidunā Salamah ؓ said:

كُنَّا نُصَلِّيْ مَعَ النَّبِيِّ ﷺ الْمَغْرِبَ إِذَا تَوَارَتْ بِالْحِجَابِ.

We used to pray maghrib ṣalāh with Nabī ﷺ when the sun disappeared beyond the horizon.[74]

❧

Ḥadīth 7
THE *SUNNAH* TIME FOR ʿISHĀ ṢALĀH

It is desirable to delay ʿishā' ṣalāh as much as possible (before one third or half of the night), because Rasūlullāh ﷺ preferred to delay this ṣalāh. Sayyidunā Abū Barzah al-Aslamī ؓ said:

---

72 *Majmaʿ al-Zawā'id*, 1:304.

73 For example: *Aḥmad* (6993); *Tirmidhī* (151).

74 *Bukhārī* (561).

وَكَانَ يَسْتَحِبُّ أَنْ يُؤَخِّرَ الْعِشَآءَ، الَّتِيْ تَدْعُوْنَهَا الْعَتَمَةَ، وَكَانَ يَكْرَهُ النَّوْمَ قَبْلَهَا وَالْحَدِيْثَ بَعْدَهَا.

He ﷺ liked to delay ʿishā' ṣalāh, which you call *ʿatamah*, and he disliked sleeping before it and talking (about worldly affairs) after it.[75]

Ḥadīth 8
THE *SUNNAH* TIME FOR FAJR ṢALĀH

The *sunnah* time for fajr ṣalāh is when the darkness disappears and it becomes quite bright, because performing fajr at this time is better than praying it in darkness.

It is narrated on the authority of Sayyidunā Rāfiʿ ibn Khadīj رضي الله عنه that Rasūlullāh ﷺ said:

نَوِّرُوْا بِصَلَاةِ الْفَجْرِ، فَإِنَّهُ أَعْظَمُ لِلْأَجْرِ.

Offer the fajr ṣalāh in light, as its reward is greater.[76]

Imām al-Tirmidhī رحمه الله (d. 379 AH) said: "The ḥadīth of Rāfiʿ ibn Khadīj رضي الله عنه is sound (*ḥasan*) and authentic (*ṣaḥīḥ*)."[77] Ḥāfiẓ Ibn Ḥajar al-ʿAsqalānī (d. 852 AH) said: "A number of ḥadīth scholars (*muḥaddiths*) authenticated this ḥadīth."[78]

In some variations of this ḥadīth, it has been narrated with the wording: أَسْفِرُوْا بِالْفَجْرِ

This has a similar meaning. In other words, perform fajr when it becomes bright. In any case, it is established from this

75 *Bukhārī* (547).

76 *Dārimī* (1218); *Tirmidhī* (154); *Abū Dāwūd* (424); *Nasā'ī* (550).

77 *Tirmidhī* (154).

78 *Fatḥ al-Bārī*, 2:69.

ḥadīth that to perform fajr when the brightness increases is better and greater in reward.

ʿAllāmah al-Shawkānī (d. 1255 AH) preferred the ḥadīth of performing fajr in brightness over the ḥadīth of performing it in darkness, because the former has been transmitted with an imperative command (*amr*).[79]

However, in the blessed month of Ramaḍān, it is better to perform fajr earlier, because this was Rasūlullāh's ﷺ practice in Ramaḍān. He ﷺ would perform fajr after finishing his pre-dawn meal (*suḥūr*). Sayyidunā Anas ؓ reports from Sayyidunā Zaid ibn Thābit ؓ that the Ṣaḥābah ؓ would eat the pre-dawn meal (*suḥūr*) with Rasūlullāh ﷺ and then perform fajr ṣalāh. The narrator of this ḥadīth asked Sayyidunā Anas ؓ how much time was there between the pre-dawn meal (*suḥūr*) and performing ṣalāh. He replied: "Around fifty to sixty verses."[80] In other words, the time required to recite fifty or sixty verses of the Qur'ān.

❧

Ḥadīth 9
THE PROHIBITIVELY REPREHENSIBLE TIMES OF ṢALĀH

There are three times when performing ṣalāh is prohibitively reprehensible (*makrūh taḥrīmī*):

1. After fajr ṣalāh until the sun has fully risen. However, after fajr ṣalāh until before sunrise, it is permissible to perform any missed (*qaḍā'*) obligatory ṣalāh;

2. During the sun's meridian at midday until ẓuhr time;

79 *Nayl al-Awṭār*, 1:248.
80 *Bukhārī* (575).

3. After ʿaṣr ṣalāh until sunset. However, before the sun begins to set, it is permissible to perform any missed obligatory ṣalāh. Once the sun begins to set [i.e., when the sun turns pale and it is possible to look at it directly], it is impermissible to perform any ṣalāh except ʿaṣr of that day.

The prohibitively reprehensible (*makrūh taḥrīmī*) times for performing ṣalāh, in the above three scenarios, are stated in the following ḥadīth in which Sayyidunā ʿAmr ibn ʿAbasah al-Sulamī ﵁ narrates:

قُلْتُ: يَانَبِيَّ اللهِ، أَخْبِرْنِيْ عَمَّا عَلَّمَكَ اللهُ وَأَجْهَلُهُ؛ أَخْبِرْنِيْ عَنِ الصَّلَاةِ. قَالَ: صَلِّ صَلَاةَ الصُّبْحِ، ثُمَّ أَقْصِرْ عَنِ الصَّلَاةِ حَتَّى تَطْلُعَ الشَّمْسُ حَتَّى تَرْتَفِعَ؛ فَإِنَّهَا تَطْلُعُ حِيْنَ تَطْلُعُ بَيْنَ قَرْنَيْ شَيْطَانٍ، وَحِيْنَئِذٍ يَسْجُدُ لَهَا الْكُفَّارُ، ثُمَّ صَلِّ؛ فَإِنَّ الصَّلَاةَ مَشْهُوْدَةٌ مَحْضُوْرَةٌ حَتَّى يَسْتَقِلَّ الظِّلُّ بِالرُّمْحِ، ثُمَّ أَقْصِرْ عَنِ الصَّلَاةِ؛ فَإِنَّ حِيْنَئِذٍ تُسْجَرُ جَهَنَّمُ، فَإِذَا أَقْبَلَ الْفَيْئُ فَصَلِّ؛ فَإِنَّ الصَّلَاةَ مَشْهُوْدَةٌ مَحْضُوْرَةٌ حَتَّى تُصَلِّيَ الْعَصْرَ، ثُمَّ أَقْصِرْ عَنِ الصَّلَاةِ حَتَّى تَغْرُبَ الشَّمْسُ؛ فَإِنَّهَا تَغْرُبُ بَيْنَ قَرْنَيْ شَيْطَانٍ، وَحِيْنَئِذٍ يَسْجُدُ لَهَا الْكُفَّارُ.

I said: "O Prophet of Allāh, tell me what Allāh has taught you and I do not know: tell me about ṣalāh." He said: 'Perform fajr ṣalāh, then refrain from ṣalāh until the sun has risen fully, because it rises when it does between the horns of Satan, and the unbelievers prostrate to it at that time. Then perform ṣalāh, as ṣalāh is witnessed and attended (by angels), till the shadow reaches the length of a lance. Then refrain from ṣalāh, as at that time Hell is heated up. Thereafter, when the shadow moves forward, perform ṣalāh, for the ṣalāh is witnessed and attended (by angels), till you perform ʿaṣr ṣalāh. Then refrain from ṣalāh till the sun sets, as it sets between the horns of Satan, and the unbelievers prostrate to it at that time.'[81]

The meaning of the sun rising and setting between Satan's horns is that when the sun rises or sets, Satan stands in front of the sun, so it appears that the sun is setting and rising between his head. The reason Satan does this is because people who worship the sun prostrate to it when it rises and sets, thus he wants to give the impression to his subordinate satans that sun-worshippers are prostrating to him. This is why the ḥadīth prohibits performing ṣalāh when the sun is rising or setting. Allāh knows best.

In any case, the aforementioned ḥadīth and other similar ḥadīths prohibit a person from performing any ṣalāh - be it supererogatory (*nafl*) or obligatory (*farḍ*) - in those three times. This prohibition also includes *taḥiyyat al-masjid.*

ʿAllāmah Amīr al-Ṣanʿānī (d. 1183 AH) wrote:

إِنَّه لَا يُصَلِّيْهِمَا مَنْ دَخَلَ الْمَسْجِدَ فِى أَوْقَاتِ الْكَرَاهَةِ.

A person entering the masjid at the reprehensible (*makrūh*) times will not perform them.[82]

Mawlānā ʿAbdullāh Rawparī* (d. 1384 AH) said, "It is not correct to perform *taḥiyyat al-masjid* after the appearance of dawn (*fajr*), just as it is not correct to perform ṣalāh during sunrise and sunset."[83]

It has been reported in some narrations that Rasūlullāh ﷺ performed two *rakʿahs* of supererogatory (*nafl*) after ʿaṣr. However, this is exclusive to Rasūlullāh ﷺ, as he forbade this practice, as stated in the ḥadīth of Sayyidunā ʿAmr ibn ʿAbasah al-Sulamī ﷺ.

81 Muslim (928).

82 *Subul al-Salām*, 1:166.

83 *Fatāwā Aḥl-i-Ḥadīth*, 1:417.

Sayyidunā ʿUmar ﷺ would severely censure a person, even in the presence of other Ṣaḥābah, who performs supererogatory (*nafl*) ṣalāh after performing ʿaṣr, to the extent that he would punish them.[84] Moreover, it is also reprehensible (*makrūh*) to perform supererogatory (*nafl*) ṣalāh on Friday during the sun's meridian at midday.

Some people consider it permissible to perform supererogatory (*nafl*) ṣalāh at that time, citing weak narrations as evidence. However, Mawlānā Sharaf al-Dīn al-Dihlawī* (d. 1961) said after accepting these narrations as weak: "It is established that performing ṣalāh during the sun's meridian at midday is prohibited, whether on Friday or any other day, because the narrations of prohibition are authentic, whilst the narrations of permissibility are weak. It is wrong to act upon weak narrations in the presence of authentic narrations."[85]

Ḥadīth 10
THE *SUNNAH* WORDING OF *ADHĀN* AND *IQĀMAH*

It is *sunnah* that the phrases of *adhān* and *iqāmah* are said in pairs, i.e., every phrase should be said twice, except for the last phrase which is to be said only once. The words of *adhān* are:

اَللهُ أَكْبَرُ ، اَللهُ أَكْبَرُ

Allāh is the Greatest. Allāh is the Greatest.

اَللهُ أَكْبَرُ ، اَللهُ أَكْبَرُ

Allāh is the Greatest. Allāh is the Greatest.

84 *ʿUmdat al-Qārī*, 5:113.

85 *Fatāwā Thanā'iyyah*, 1:543; *Fatāwā ʿUlamā'-i-Ḥadīth*, 4:162.

أَشْهَدُ أَنْ لَّا إِلَٰهَ إِلَّا اللهُ

I testify that there is no deity besides Allāh.

أَشْهَدُ أَنْ لَّا إِلَٰهَ إِلَّا اللهُ

I testify that there is no deity besides Allāh.

أَشْهَدُ أَنَّ مُحَمَّدًا رَّسُوْلُ اللهِ

I testify that Muḥammad is the Messenger of Allāh.

أَشْهَدُ أَنَّ مُحَمَّدًا رَّسُوْلُ اللهِ

I testify that Muḥammad is the Messenger of Allāh.

حَيَّ عَلَى الصَّلَاةِ

Come to ṣalāh.

حَيَّ عَلَى الصَّلَاةِ

Come to ṣalāh.

حَيَّ عَلَى الْفَلَاحِ

Come to success.

حَيَّ عَلَى الْفَلَاحِ

Come to success.

اَللهُ أَكْبَرُ ، اَللهُ أَكْبَرُ

Allāh is the Greatest. Allāh is the Greatest.

لَا إِلَٰهَ إِلَّا اللهُ

There is no deity besides Allāh.[86]

---

86 Taken from *Ṣalāt al-Rasūl*, p. 153-154, by Mawlānā Muḥammad Ṣādiq Siyālkawtī. Also see: *al-Maṭālib al-ʿĀliyah*, 1:365; *Itḥāf al-Khiyarat al-Maharah*, 2:21; *Al-Musnad al-Mustakhraj ʿalā Ṣaḥīḥ Muslim* of Abū Nuʿaym, 2:4.

The *iqāmah* is the same as the *adhān*. However, the following addition will be said twice after *ḥayya ʿala 'l-falāḥ*:

قَدْ قَامَتِ الصَّلٰوةُ

Ṣalāh has been established.

Similarly, in fajr *adhān*, the following phrase will be said twice after *ḥayya ʿala 'l-falāḥ*:

اَلصَّلَوةُ خَيْرٌ مِّنَ النَّوْمِ

Ṣalāh is better than sleep.

It is established from several ḥadīths that the phrases of *adhān* and *iqāmah* should be said twice. Sayyidunā ʿAbdullah ibn Zayd ﷺ saw a dream in which he was taught the *adhān* and the *iqāmah*. Rasūlullāh ﷺ affirmed this dream and instructed Sayyidunā Bilāl ﷺ to say the *adhān* and the *iqāmah* according to the method Sayyidunā ʿAbdullāh ibn Zayd ﷺ was taught in his dream. The phrases in this *adhān* and *iqāmah* were repeated.

The famous Tābiʿī, ʿAbd al-Raḥmān ibn Abī Laylā ﷺ said:

حَدَّثَنَا أَصْحَابُ رَسُوْلِ اللهِ ﷺ أَنَّ عَبْدَ اللهِ بْنَ زَيْدٍ الْأَنْصَارِىَّ ﷺ جَاءَ إِلَى النَّبِيِّ ﷺ فَقَالَ: يَارَسُوْلَ اللهِ؛ رَأَيْتُ فِي الْمَنَامِ كَأَنَّ رَجْلًا قَامَ، وَعَلَيْهِ بُرْدَانِ أَخْضَرَانِ عَلَى جِذْمَةِ حَائِطٍ، فَأَذَّنَ مَثْنَى، وَأَقَامَ مَثْنَى. وَفِيْ رِوَايَةٍ: ثُمَّ قَالَ فِيْ آخِرِ أَذَانِهِ: اَللهُ اَكْبَرُ اَللهُ اَكْبَرُ، لَا إِلَهَ إِلَّا اللهُ، ثُمَّ أَمْهَلَ شَيْئًا، ثُمَّ قَامَ، فَقَالَ مِثْلَ الَّذِىْ قَالَ، غَيْرَ أَنَّهُ زَادَ: قَدْ قَامَتِ الصَّلَوةُ.

The Ṣaḥābah of Rasūlullāh ﷺ narrated to us that ʿAbdullāh ibn Zayd al-Anṣārī ﷺ came to Nabī ﷺ and said, "O Rasūlullāh, I saw a dream as though a man wearing two green shawls stood on a wall, and he performed the *adhān* and the *iqāmah*, saying each phrase twice."[87]

In one narration: He then said at the end of his *adhān*:

اَللّٰهُ اَكْبَرُ اَللّٰهُ اَكْبَرُ، لَا إِلَهَ إِلَّا اَللّٰهُ.

He then paused for a while, whereafter he stood and said (the *iqāmah*) like his *adhān*, except he added the words *qad qāmat'l-ṣālah* قَدْ قَامَتِ الصَّلٰوةُ.

In this ḥadīth, it is also mentioned towards the end of the narration that when Sayyidunā ʿAbdullāh ibn Zayd ؓ narrated the dream to Rasūlullāh ﷺ, he ﷺ instructed him to teach the words to Sayyidunā Bilāl ؓ who then performed the *adhān* and the *iqāmah* by saying each phrase twice.

Imām Ibn Daqīq al-ʿĪd (d. 703 AH) and Imām Ibn Rajab (d. 785 AH) said regarding this ḥadīth:

هَذَا رِجَالُ الصَّحِيْحَيْنِ وَمُتَّصِلٌ عَلَى مَذْهَبِ الْجَمَاعَةِ فِيْ عَدَالَةِ الصَّحَابَةِ، وَإِنَّ جَهَالَةَ أَسْمَائِهِمْ لَا تَضُرُّ.

These are the narrators of Bukhārī and Muslim, and its chain, according to the opinion of the vast majority (of ḥadīth scholars) with respect to the Ṣaḥābah being reliable, is connected (*muttaṣil*), and their names being unknown is of no harm.[88]

ʿAllāmah Ibn Ḥazm al-Ẓāhirī (d. 456 AH) and Shaykh Nāṣir al-Dīn Albānī (d. 1420 AH) clearly stated that this ḥadīth is rigorously authentic.[89]

Some non-muqallids object to this ḥadīth because of the

87 *Muṣannaf Ibn Abī Shaybah*, 1:331; Bayhaqī's *al-Sunan al-Kubrā*, 1:420; *al-Muḥallā*, 3:97.

88 *Naṣb al-Rāyah*, 1:267; Ibn Rajab's *Fatḥ al-Bārī*, 3:407.

89 *Al-Muḥallā*, 3:98. *Aḥkām al-Adhān wa 'l-Iqāmah*, p. 85.

tadlīs[90] of Aʿmash, one of its narrators. However, Mawlānā ʿAbd al-Raḥmān Mubārakpūri clearly stated, quoting Imām al-Ḥalabī, that the *tadlīs* of Aʿmash is not harmful,[91] especially when Imām Shuʿbah and others have corroborated his ḥadīth.[92]

Furthermore, this ḥadīth is strengthened by several authentic narrations.[93] Nawāb Ṣiddiq Ḥasan Khān (d. 1307 AH) has acknowledged that the narrations regarding *iqāmah* phrases being repeated are authentic.[94]

Some narrations report the phrases of *iqāmah* to be single, i.e., every phrase should be said once. However, the ḥadīths stating *iqāmah* phrases being repeated are more authentic. ʿAllāmah al-Shawkānī (d. 1255 AH) preferred the narrations of *iqāmah* phrases being repeated over the narrations that state them to be said once. He writes:

إِذَا عَرَفْتَ هَذَا تَبَيَّنَ لَكَ أَنَّ أَحَادِيْثَ تَثْنِيَةِ الْإِقَامَةِ صَالِحَةٌ لِلْاِحْتِجَاجِ بِهَا لِمَا سَلَفْنَاهُ، وَأَحَادِيْثُ إِفْرَادِ الْإِقَامَةِ وَإِنْ كَانَتْ أَصَحَّ مِنْهَا لِكَثْرَةِ طُرُقِهَا فِي الصَّحِيْحَيْنِ لَكِنَّ أَحَادِيْثَ التَّثْنِيَةِ مُشْتَمِلَةٌ عَلَى الزِّيَادَةِ، فَالْمَصِيْرُ إِلَيْهَا لَازِمٌ، لَاسِيَّمَا مَعَ تَأَخُّرِ بَعْضِهَا كَمَا عَرَّفْنَاكَ.

Once you have understood this, it will be clear to you that the ḥadīths on *iqāmah* phrases being repeated are suitable as evidence, due to what we previously mentioned. The

---

90 *Tadlīs* is when a narrator in a chain of transmission mentions the name of the narrator above his teacher, instead of mentioning his own teacher first, and he uses such words which give the impression that he heard the ḥadīth from his teacher's teacher. For example: he says: from such-and-such عَنْ فُلَانٍ. A narrator who conceals in this manner is called a '*mudallis*'.

91 *Maqālāt Mubārakpūrī*, p. 368.

92 *Abū Dāwūd* (506-507); *Ibn Khuzaymah*, 1:170; *Sharḥ Maʿānī al-Āthār*, 1:93; *Aḥkām al-Adhān wa 'l-Iqāmah*, p. 51.

93 *Sharḥ Maʿānī al-Āthār*, 1:94; *Ṣaḥīḥ Abī ʿAwānah*, 2:223; *Majmaʿ al-Zawā'id*, 1:230-231; *al-Dirāyah*, 1:115; Abū Nuʿaym's *Maʿrifat al-Ṣaḥābah*, 3:149.

94 *Al-Rawḍah al-Nadiyyah*, 1:79.

> narrations of *iqāmah* phrases being said once, albeit they are more authentic due to their many chains in the two *Ṣaḥīḥs* (i.e., Bukhārī and Muslim). However, the ḥadīths of *iqāmah* phrases being repeated contains additional wording. Therefore, taking those ḥadīths will be necessary, especially when some of them being later (from the practice of Rasūlullāh ﷺ), as we have previously explained to you.[95]

Nawāb Ṣiddiq Ḥasan (d. 1307 AH) and his son, Mawlānā Nūr al-Ḥasan (d. 1336 AH), have both acknowledged that repeating the phrases of the *iqāmah* is preferable by way of principle.[96]

It should be clear from the aforementioned narrations, alongside others, that the phrases of the *adhān* and the *iqāmah* are repeated. However, none of them mention *tarjīʿ*, which means to first say the *shahādatayn* phrases quietly and then repeating them loudly. Also, there is a ḥadīth transmitted from Sayyidunā Abū Maḥdhūrah ﷺ, who is the only narrator of the *tarjīʿ* narration, in which there is no *tarjīʿ* in the *adhān* or the *iqāmah*, and the phrases are in pairs.[97] This ḥadīth is totally authentic in light of the accepted principles of non-muqallid scholars.[98] This also invalidates the view of some non-muqallids who claim that the phrases of the *iqāmah* being repeated is only a *sunnah* when there is *tarjīʿ*. Shaykh al-Albānī has strongly refuted this opinion, and he clearly states that repeating the phrases of the *adhān* and the *iqāmah* without *tarjīʿ* is established from ḥadīths.[99] Shaykh al-Albānī also strongly refuted the view of Ibn Ḥazm who said that repeating the phrases of *iqāmah* is abrogated (*mansūkh*).[100]

---

95 *Nayl al-Awṭār*, 1:262.
96 *Al-Rawḍah al-Nadiyyah*, 1:79. *ʿArf al-Jādī*, p. 25.
97 *Al-Musnad al-Mustakhraj ʿalā Saḥīḥ Muslim* (835).
98 Monthly *Al-Ḥadīth*, volume 17: p. 8.
99 *Aḥkām al-Adhān wa 'l-Iqāmah*, p. 87-88.
100 Ibid.

Some extreme non-muqallids have gone to the extent of saying that repeating the phrases of the *iqāmah* is against the Sunnah and impermissible, whereas their great researcher, Mawlānā ʿAbd al-Raḥmān Mubārakpūrī (d. 1352 AH) clearly states that both ways of performing the *iqāmah* are permissible, and a person can choose any one of them. He says:

حَمَلَ بَعْضُهُمْ عَلَى الْإِبَاحَةِ وَالتَّخْيِيْرِ، فَهُوَ الْحَقُّ.

Some scholars have interpreted this as permissibility and choice, and this is the correct view.[101]

Mawlānā Muḥammad Ismāʿīl Salafī* (d. 1387 AH) said: "If there is no repetition of the *shahādatayn* in the *adhān*, *takbīr* (*Allāhu akbar*) is said four times in the *iqāmah* (as in *adhān*) and the *shahādatayn* are said twice, this is also correct."[102]

Ḥadīth 11

THE *SUNNAH* WAY FOR MEN TO RAISE THE HANDS FOR THE OPENING *TAKBĪR* AND THE *SUNNAH* WORDING OF *THANĀ'*

When a person makes intention for ṣalāh while facing the *qiblah*, he should begin with the opening *takbīr* (*takbīr taḥrīmah*), whilst raising both hands to the ears, and then fold his hands beneath the navel and recite the praise (*thanā'*).

Sayyidunā Anas ibn Mālik ﷺ said:

كَانَ رَسُوْلُ اللهِ ﷺ إِذَا افْتَتَحَ الصَّلَاةَ كَبَّرَ، ثُمَّ رَفَعَ يَدَيْهِ حَتَّى يُحَاذِيَ إِبْهَامَيْهِ

101 *Ibkār al-Minan*, p. 89.

102 *Rasūl-i-Akram* ﷺ *kī Namāz*, p. 32.

أُذُنَيْهِ ثُمَّ يَقُوْلُ: سُبْحَانَكَ اللَّهُمَّ وَبِحَمْدِكَ، وَ تَبَارَكَ اسْمُكَ، وَتَعَالَى جَدُّكَ، وَلَا إِلَهَ غَيْرُكَ.

When Rasūlullāh ﷺ would start his ṣalāh, he would say the takbīr, then raise both hands until his thumbs were parallel to his ears, and then he would read: *Pure are You, O Allāh, and with Your praise. Blessed is Your name, lofty is Your majesty, and there is no deity besides You.*[103]

Imām al-Dāraquṭnī and Imām al-Ḥaythamī both classed all the narrators of the abovementioned ḥadīth to be reliable.[104] One of the narrators of this ḥadīth, Abū Khālid al-Aḥmar, being a *mudallis* (one who commits *tadlīs*) is not proven from Imām Aḥmad, whilst his teacher, Ḥumayd al-Ṭawīl's *tadlīs* is not considered harmful according to Mawlānā Mubārakpūrī.[105] Also, Ḥusayn al-ʿAjlī's being disputed (in terms of reliability) means his narrations are sound (*ḥasan*) as acknowledged by non-muqallid scholars.[106]

Furthermore, Ḥāfiẓ Ibn Ḥajar al-ʿAsqalānī clearly stated this ḥadīth has two other chains which are good to further support it.[107] Shaykh al-Albānī authenticated the chain of this ḥadīth, and deemed the objections (of Abū Ḥātim and others) on the authenticity of the ḥadīth to be negligible.[108] Mawlānā ʿAbd al-Ra'ūf Sindhū* also regarded the ḥadīth as authentic.[109]

Mawlānā ʿAbd al-Rằūf stated that reading *thanā'* after *takbīr taḥrīmah* is proven from several Ṣaḥābah other than Sayyidunā

---

103 *Dāraquṭnī* (1135); *al-Muʿjam al-Awsaṭ* (3039); Ṭabarānī's *Kitāb al-Duʿā'* (505, 506).

104 *Naṣb al-Rāyah*, 1:320; *al-Dirāyah*, 1:129; *Majmaʿ al-Zawā'id*, 2:107.

105 *Maqālāt Mubārakpūrī*, p. 368.

106 *Khayr al-Kalām*, p. 238.

107 *Al-Dirāyah*, 1:129.

108 *Irwā' al-Ghalīl*, 2:50-52; *Silsilat al-Aḥādīth al-Ṣaḥīḥah* (2996).

109 *Al-Qawl al-Maqbūl*, p. 347.

Anas: Sayyida ʿĀ'ishah, Sayyidunā Jābir, Sayyidunā Abū Saʿīd, Sayyidunā Ibn Masʿūd, Sayyidunā Ḥakīm ibn ʿUmayr and Sayyidunā Wāthilah ﷺ are amongst those who have narrated this from Rasūlullāh ﷺ.[110]

It should be noted that after saying *takbīr taḥrīmah*, there are several different prayers reported from Rasūlullāh ﷺ. However, it is best to recite the words of the aforementioned *thanā'*, because Rasūlullāh ﷺ would mostly recite this after *takbīr taḥrīmah*. Hence, Shaykh al-Islām Majd al-Dīn Ibn Taymiyyah (d. 652 AH) said that this is better and it is the one which Rasūlullāh ﷺ would read habitually.[111]

Sayyidunā ʿUmar ﷺ, and the Rightly-guided Caliphs (*al-khulafā' al-rāshidūn*), would also be very particular about reciting this *thanā'*, and the rest of the Ṣaḥābah were in agreement with them.[112]

As for raising the hands to the ears when saying *takbīr taḥrīmah*, this is proven from numerous authentic ḥadīths, apart from the aforementioned ḥadīth.[113]

Mawlānā Muḥammad Gawndlawī* said that raising the hands to the ears is established, as proven from authentic ḥadīths.[114]

---

110 *Al-Qawl al-Maqbūl*, p. 346-348.

111 *Al-Muntaqā*, 1:370.

112 *Al-Muḥallā*, 4:64; *ʿAwn al-Maʿbūd*, 2:153.

113 *Al-Muʿjam al-Kabīr* (4982-4983, 4986, 4988-4989, 4994); *Aḥmad* (16197, 18906); *Abū Dāwūd* (728); *Nasā'ī* (884); *Mustadrak al-Ḥākim* (822).

114 *Al-Taḥqīq al-Rāsikh*, p. 47.

Ḥadīth 12

IT IS *SUNNAH* FOR WOMEN TO RAISE THE HANDS TO THE CHEST WITH THE OPENING *TAKBĪR*

It is *sunnah* for women to raise their hands to their chest when saying the opening takbir, i.e., *takbīr taḥrīmah*. Sayyidunā Wā'il ibn Ḥujr ﷺ said:

قَالَ لِيْ رَسُوْلُ اللهِ ﷺ: يَا وَائِلَ بْنَ حُجْرٍ! إِذَا صَلَّيْتَ، فَاجْعَلْ يَدَيْكَ حِذَاءَ أُذُنَيْكَ، وَالْمَرْأَةُ تَجْعَلُ يَدَيْهَا حِذَاءَ ثَدْيَيْهَا.

Rasūlullāh ﷺ said to me, "O Wā'il ibn Ḥujr! When you perform ṣalāh, raise your hands to your ears, and a woman will raise her hands to her chest (close to her shoulders)."[115]

Imām Nūr al-Dīn al-Ḥaythamī (d. 807 AH) stated after citing the aforementioned ḥadīth: "It contains Umm Yaḥyā bint ʿAbd al-Jabbār whom I do not recognise, and the rest of its narrators are reliable."[116]

Mawlānā ʿAbdullāh Rawparī said regarding Umm Yaḥyā ibn ʿAbd al-Jabbār (whose name is Kishsha):[117] Umm Yaḥyā narrates from Anas and ʿAbdullāh ibn ʿUmar ʿUmarī narrates from Umm Yaḥyā. Ḥāfiẓ Ibn Ḥajar did not say she is unknown. From this explanation, we can understand that the ḥadīth contains a slight discrepancy, which can easily be resolved with slight support."[118]

From the above statement of Mawlānā ʿAbdullāh Rawparī, we learn two things:

115 *Al-Muʿjam al-Kabīr* (28).

116 *Majmaʿ al-Zawā'id*, 2:103.

117 Ibn Mākūlā's *Al-Ikmāl*, 7:124; Ibn Ḥajar's *Tabṣīr al-Muntabih*, 3:1185.

118 *Fatāwā Ahl-i-Ḥadīth*, 1:314.

1. Umm Yaḥyā is not unknown
2. Her ḥadīth is suitable as evidence after some support.

Based on this, the aforementioned ḥadīth can also be used as evidence, because it is supported by numerous narrations. Imām ʿAṭā' ibn Abī Rabāḥ (d. 114 AH), Imām Ḥammād ibn Abī Sulaymān (d. 120 AH), Imām al-Zuhrī (d. 124 AH), and other great jurists from the Tābiʿūn ﷺ said that when a woman says the *takbīr taḥrīmah*, she should raise her hands until her chest. The jurist amongst the Tābiʿūn, Ḥafṣah bint Sīrīn (d. 101 AH) would also practice the raising of the hands to the chest when saying the *takbīr taḥrīmah*.[119]

In addition to this, Mawlānā Waḥīd al-Zamān (d. 1338 AH) stated that from the issues in which a man's ṣalāh differs to that of a woman's ṣalāh is that a woman will raise her hands to her chest when saying the *takbīr taḥrīmah*.[120]

Ḥadīth 13
IT IS *SUNNAH* TO FASTEN THE HANDS BELOW THE NAVEL IN *QIYĀM*

It is *sunnah* for a man when standing (*qiyām*) in ṣalāh to fold the right hand over the left hand beneath the navel.

Sayyidunā Wā'il ibn Ḥujr ؓ narrates:

رَأَيْتُ النَّبِيَّ ﷺ يَضَعُ يَمِيْنَهُ عَلَى شِمَالِهِ فِي الصَّلٰوةِ تَحْتَ السُّرَّةِ.

I saw Nabī ﷺ placing his right hand over his left hand beneath the navel in ṣalāh.[121]

119 *Muṣannaf Ibn Abī Shaybah*, 1:270.

120 *Kanz al-Ḥaqā'iq*, p. 22; *Nuzul al-Abrār*, 1:85.

121 *Muṣannaf Ibn Abī Shaybah*, 1:427.

ʿAllāmah Qāsim ibn Quṭlūbughā (d. 879 AH) and Mawlānā ʿAbd al-Raḥmān Mubārakpūrī said regarding the aforementioned ḥadīth that its chain is good (*jayyid*).[122]

In most of the manuscripts of *Muṣannaf Ibn Abī Shaybah*, this ḥadīth has been transmitted with the words below the navel (*taḥt al-surrah*). ʿAllāmah Muḥammad Hāshim Sindhī (d. 1174 AH) ﷺ has mentioned in his book *Tarṣī al-Durrah Maʿa Dirham al-Ṣurrah* that three manuscripts have the words "below the navel (*taḥt al-surrah*)".[123] Similarly, the ḥadīth in the manuscript of Mawlānā Shams al-Ḥaqq ʿAẓīmābādī (d. 1329 AH) also contains these words.[124]

However, some of the manuscripts of Muṣannaf Ibn Abī Shaybah do not have the words "below the navel (*taḥt al-surrah*)", but this does not render the authentic manuscripts with these words to be interpolated or unreliable.

Mawlānā Bashīr Sayswānī* (d. 1326 AH) and Mawlānā ʿAbd al-Rahmān Mubārakpūrī (d. 1353 AH) clearly state that in the books of ḥadīth, there are many narrations which exist in some manuscripts but not in others. However, no one considers them to be forged or unreliable.[125] Moreoever, this ḥadīth is supported by a number of other ḥadīths, especially the narration reported by Sayyidunā ʿAlī ﷺ:

السُّنَّةُ وَضْعُ الْكَفِّ عَلَى الْكَفِّ فِي الصَّلَاةِ تَحْتَ السُّرَّةِ.

The *sunnah* is to place one hand over the other in ṣalāh below the navel.[126]

This narration has been authenticated by Imām Ḍiyā' al-Dīn

122 *Tuḥfat al-Aḥwadhī*, 1:214.

123 *Tarṣī al-Durrah Maʿa Dirham al-Ṣurrah*, p. 82, Maktabah Imdādiyyah, Multan edition.

124 Ibid, p. 7.

125 *Al-Burhān al-ʿUjāb*, p. 263; *Taḥqīq al-Kalām*, 2:48-49.

126 *Abū Dāwūd* (756, 758); *al-Muḥallā*, 4:74; *al-Tamhīd*, 7:247.

al-Maqdisī (d. 643 AH) in *al-Mukhtārah*.[127] This is evidence of its authenticity according to non-muqallid scholars, as will be discussed under ḥadīth thirty.

The teacher of Imām al-Bukhārī, Imām Isḥāq ibn Rāhwayh (d. 308 AH) said:

تَحْتَ السُّرَّةِ أَقْوَى فِي الْحَدِيْثِ وَأَقْرَبُ إِلَى التَّوَاضُعِ.

(Fastening the hands) below the navel is stronger from a ḥadīth perspective and closer to humility.[128]

Nawāb Siddīque Ḥasan Khān (d. 1307 AH) and his son, Nawāb Nūr al-Ḥasan (d. 1336 AH), both acknowledged that the ḥadīths with the words below the navel are authentic and free from criticism.[129] They also stated that folding the hands below the navel is reported from several Ṣaḥābah.[130]

In several narrations it has been mentioned that the ṣalāh of a woman is different to that of a man in certain aspects. Based on these narrations, the jurists said that a woman, when standing in ṣalāh, will place her hands on her chest instead of below the navel, as this is more concealing for a woman.

In the state of *qawmah* (standing up straight after *rukūʿ*), both men and women should leave their hands on their sides and not hold them below the navel or on the chest. This has been the constant practice of the Ummah for over fourteen hundred years. Some of the non-muqallids place their hands on their chest in *qawmah*, whereas their reputable scholars such as ʿAllāmah Waḥīd al-Zamān, Shaykh Albānī, Shaykh Muḥibullāh

127 (771, 772)

128 Ibn al-Mundhir's *al-Awsaṭ*, 3:243.

129 *Al-Rawḍah al-Nadiyyah*, 1:97, 98; *ʿArf al-Jādī*, p. 25.

130 Ibid.

Rāshidī* and others all considered this to be a misguided innovation (*bidʿah ḍalālah*).[131]

❧

Ḥadīth 14
IT IS *SUNNAH* TO RECITE *TASMIYAH* QUIETLY BEFORE STARTING *SURAT AL-FĀTIḤAH*

After *thanā'*, the following *taʿawwudh* will be recited quietly:

أَعُوْذُ بِاللهِ مِنَ الشَّيْطٰنِ الرَّجِيْمِ.

Similarly, the *tasmiyah* should also be said quietly, as this is the *sunnah* practice. Sayyidunā Anas ؓ said:

صَلَّيْتُ خَلْفَ رَسُوْلِ اللهِ ﷺ وَأَبِيْ بَكْرٍ وعُمَرَ وَعُثْمَانَ ؓ، فَلَمْ أَسْمَعْ أَحَدًا مِّنْهُمْ يَجْهَرُ بِـ﴿بِسْمِ اللهِ الرَّحْمٰنِ الرَّحِيْمِ﴾

I prayed ṣalāh behind Rasūlullāh ﷺ, Abū Bakr, ʿUmar and ʿUthmān ؓ, but I did not hear any of them read *bismi'llāhi 'r-raḥmāni 'r-raḥīm* loudly.[132]

Imām al-Zaylaʿī (d. 763 AH) said the narrators of this ḥadīth are all reliable and narrators of *Ṣaḥīh al-Bukhārī*.[133]

Both Imām Ibn Khuzaymah (d. 311 AH) and Imām Ibn Ḥibbān (d. 354 AH) have mentioned this ḥadīth in their *ṣaḥīh* compilations.[134] Mawlānā ʿAbd al-Ra'ūf stated that Ibn Khuzaymah and

131 *Nuzul al-Abrār*, 1:79; *Ṣifat Ṣalāt al-Nabīyy*, p. 139; *Maqālāt Rāshidiyyah*, 1:87.

132 *Nasā'ī* (908); Abū Nuʿaym's *Musnad al-Imām Abī Ḥanīfah*, p. 132.

133 *Naṣb al-Rāyah*, 1:327.

134 *Ibn Khuzaymah* (495, 496, 497); *al-Iḥsān bi-Tartīb Ṣaḥīh Ibn Ḥibbān* (1795).

Ibn Ḥibbān have only mentioned those ḥadīths in their books which they consider authentic.[135]

Moreover, it is established from Sayyidunā ʿAlī ؓ that he, like the Rightly-guided Caliphs (*al-khulafā' al-rāshidūn*) ؓ before him, would recite the *tasmiyah* quietly.[136] On the other hand, there is no authentic ḥadīth which states that *tasmiyah* should be said loudly.

Mawlānā ʿAbd al-Ra'ūf has written: "In conclusion, there is no explicit, authentic ḥadīth which states that *tasmiyah* should be read aloud. Therefore, it should be read quietly. Shaykh al-Islām Ibn Taymiyyah ؒ said that the scholars of ḥadīth unanimously agreed that there is no explicit, authentic narration on reading *tasmiyah* loudly. The famous compilers of the *Sunan* collections, such as Imāms Abū Dāwūd, Tirmidhī, Nasā'ī and others, have not reported any narration regarding this.

Reading *tasmiyah* loudly has been mentioned in fabricated narrations by Thaʿlabī, Māwardī and exegetes of their rank, or you will find these fabricated narrations in the books of jurists who did not differentiate between authentic and fabricated narrations, rather they would use all types of narrations as evidences."[137]

❧

135 *Al-Qawl al-Maqbūl*, p. 44.

136 *Al-Istidhkār*, 1:458.

137 *Al-Qawl al-Maqbūl*, p. 237 (first edition); p. 355-356 (fourth edition).

Ḥadīth 15
THE METHOD OF RECITATION (*QIRĀ'AH*) IN OBLIGATORY ṢALĀH FOR AN IMĀM AND A PERSON PERFORMING ṢALĀH ON THEIR OWN

The method of recitation in obligatory (*farḍ*) ṣalāh, both for an imām and for one who is praying individually, is that they will recite *Sūrat al-Fātiḥah* and any other *sūrah* in the two *rakʿahs* of fajr, as well as in the first two *rakʿahs* of ẓuhr, ʿaṣr, maghrib and ʿishā'. However, in the final two *rakʿahs* of ẓuhr, ʿaṣr, ʿishā' and in the third *rakʿah* of maghrib, they will only recite *Surat al-Fātiḥah.*

Sayyidunā Abū Qatādah ﵁ has reported:

أَنَّ النَّبِيَّ ﷺ كَانَ يَقْرَأُ فِي الظُّهْرِ الْأُوْلَيَيْنِ بِأُمِّ الْكِتَابِ وَسُوْرَتَيْنِ، وَفِي الرَّكْعَتَيْنِ الْأُخْرَيَيْنِ بِأُمِّ الْكِتَابِ، وَيُسْمِعُنَا الْآيَةَ، وَيُطَوِّلُ فِي الرَّكْعَةِ الْأُوْلَى مَالَا يُطِيْلُ فِي الرَّكْعَةِ الثَّانِيَةِ، وَهَكَذَا فِي الْعَصْرِ، وَهَكَذَا فِي الصُّبْحِ.

Nabī ﷺ used to recite *Sūrat al-Fātiḥah* followed by another *sūrah* in the first two *rakʿahs* of the ẓuhr ṣalāh, and he would recite (only) *Sūrat al-Fātiḥah* in the last two *rakʿahs* of ẓuhr ṣalāh. He would (sometimes) read a verse audibly, and he used to prolong the first *rakʿah* more than the second. He would do the same in the ʿaṣr and fajr ṣalāhs."[138]

In the aforementioned ḥadīth, the narrator has only mentioned ẓuhr, ʿaṣr and fajr as an example. However, the same will also apply in maghrib and ʿishā', even though it is not mentioned in the ḥadīth. Thus, in the first two *rakʿahs* of maghrib and ʿishā', a person will recite *Sūrat al-Fātiḥah* followed by a *sūrah*, and in the third *rakʿah* of maghrib and in the last

138 *Bukhārī* (776); *Muslim* (944).

two *rakʿahs* of ʿishā', he will only recite *Sūrat al-Fātiḥah.* In the last two *rakʿahs* of an obligatory (*farḍ*) ṣalāh, it is only desirable (*mustaḥabb*) to recite *Surat al-Fātiḥah*, as reported from Sayyidunā ʿAlī, Sayyidunā ʿAbdullāh ibn Masʿūd and others ﷺ.[139] Furthermore, this is also supported by the raised (*marfūʿ*) narration reported by Sayyidunā Saʿd ibn Abī Waqqāṣ ﷺ.[140]

It should be noted that the aforesaid method and ruling is only for obligatory (*farḍ*) ṣalāhs. It is not for *sunnah* or supererogatory (*nafl*) ṣalāhs, in which one must recite *Sūrat al-Fātiḥah*, as well as from another *sūrah*, in all of the *rakʿahs*, because each set of two *rakʿahs* therein is regarded as a separate and independent ṣalāh.

Mawlānā Muḥammad Yūnus al-Dihlawī* (d. 1388 AH) said it is necessary to join a *sūrah* or a few verses with *Sūrat al-Fātiḥah* in all of the *rakʿahs* of *sunnah* and supererogatory (*nafl*) ṣalāhs, and it is permissible to suffice upon *Sūrat al-Fātiḥah* in the last two *rakʿahs* of obligatory (*farḍ*) ṣalāhs.[141]

❧

Ḥadīth 16
RECITING IS PROHIBITED FOR A FOLLOWER (*MUQTADĪ*)

The method and ruling of recitation, explained under ḥadīth fifteen, is for both the imām and one who is performing ṣalāh on their own. However, for the follower (*muqtadī*), it is not permissible to recite *Sūrat al-Fātiḥah* or any other *sūrah*, but rather they will remain silent. This ruling will apply for the

139 *Muṣannaf ʿAbd al-Razzāq*, 2:65; *Muṣannaf Ibn Abī Shaybah*, 1:408; *al-Muʿjam al-Kabīr*, 7:3376.
140 *Bukhārī* (755); *ʿUmdat al-Qārī*, 6:12,
141 *Fatāwā ʿUlamā'-i-Ḥadīth*, 3:96.

follower (*muqtadī*) in both the louḍ ṣalāhs (fajr, maghrib and ʿishā') and the silent ṣalāhs (ẓuhr and ʿaṣr).

Allāh Most High says:

وَإِذَا قُرِئَ الْقُرْآنُ فَاسْتَمِعُوْا لَهُ وَأَنْصِتُوْا لَعَلَّكُمْ تُرْحَمُوْنَ

When the Qur'ān is recited, listen to it and be silent, so that you may be shown mercy.[142]

This is further supported by the following ḥadīth of Sayyidunā Abū Mūsā al-Ashʿarī ﵁:

إِنَّ رَسُوْلَ اللهِ ﷺ خَطَبَنَا، فَبَيَّنَ لَنَا سُنَّتَنَا وَعَلَّمَنَا صَلَاتَنَا، فَقَالَ: إِذَا صَلَّيْتُمْ فَأَقِيْمُوْا صُفُوْفَكُمْ، ثُمَّ لِيَؤُمَّكُمْ أَحَدُكُمْ، فَإِذَا كَبَّرَ فَكَبِّرُوْا، وَإِذَا قَرَأَ فَأَنْصِتُوْا، وَإِذَا قَرَأَ (غَيْرِ الْمَغْضُوْبِ عَلَيْهِمْ وَلَا الضَّالِّيْنَ)، فَقُوْلُوْا آمِيْنَ.

Rasūlullāh ﷺ addressed us, and explained to us our *sunnah* practices and taught us our ṣalāh. He said: 'When you perform (congregational) ṣalāh, straighten your rows, then one of you should lead. When he (i.e., the imām) says the takbīr, say the takbīr; when he recites, remain silent; and when he recites: غَيْرِ الْمَغْضُوْبِ عَلَيْهِمْ وَلَا الضَّالِّيْنَ say *āmīn*.'[143]

Imām Ibn Taymiyyah (d. 728 AH) said that the aforementioned ḥadīth has been authenticated by the likes of Imām Aḥmad, Imām Muslim and Imām Isḥāq ﵏. Hence, any criticism on the ḥadīth will have no effect.[144] Imām Ibn al-Mundhir (d. 318 AH) deemed objections on the authenticity of the ḥadīth to be insignificant.[145] Furthermore, a similar narration has been transmitted from Sayyidunā Abū Hurayrah ﵁. Imām

---

142 Qur'ān, 7:204.

143 *Muslim* (903); *Ṣaḥīḥ Abī ʿAwānah* (1339, 1341)

144 *Rasā'il Dīniyyah Salafiyyah*, p. 54, quoted in *Namāz-i-Payambar* ﷺ, p. 139.

145 *Al-Awsaṭ*, 3:261.

al-Nasā'ī (d. 303 AH) has mentioned this ḥadīth in his *Sunan*, and regarded it as commentary for the abovementioned Qur'ānic verse.[146]

Mawlānā ʿAbd al-Ra'ūf Sindhū has written regarding the narration of Sayyidunā Abū Hurayrah ﷺ: "This ḥadīth is authentic. Imām Muslim in his *Ṣaḥīh*, Ibn Ḥazm in his *al-Muḥallā* (3:240), al-Mundhirī in *Mukhtaṣar al-Sunan* (1:313) and Ibn al-Turkumānī in *al-Jawhar al-Naqiyy* (2:152) have authenticated this ḥadīth."[147]

In both narrations, the follower (*muqtadī*) is instructed to remain silent until the end of *Surat al-Fātiḥah*, and permitted only to say *āmīn*. This is clear evidence that the follower (*muqtadī*) is prohibited from recitation of *Sūrat al-Fātiḥah*.

The senior scholar Mawlānā Muḥammad Gawndlawī (d. 1405 AH) said: "We believe that the issue of reciting *Sūrat al-Fātiḥah* behind the imām is a subsidiary issue. Whoever does research to the best of their ability, concluding that reciting *Sūrat al-Fātiḥah* is not compulsory in the loud and quiet ṣalāhs, and then acts upon his research, his ṣalāh will not be void."[148]

He also writes: "If someone does not recite *Sūrat al-Fātiḥah* behind the imām on the basis of his research, his ṣalāh will be valid."[149]

Mawlānā Irshād al-Ḥaqq al-Atharī* said: "From the era of Imām al-Bukhārī until recent times, no claim has been made in the works of the erudite scholars of the Ahl-i-ḥadīth that the ṣalāh of one who does not recite *Sūrat al-Fātiḥah* is void or that he is considered as one who does not perform ṣalāh, and so forth."[150]

146 *Nasā'ī* (923, 924)

147 *Al-Qawl al-Maqbūl*, p. 451.

148 *Khayr al-Kalām*, p. 33.

149 Ibid, p. 245.

150 *Tawḍīḥ al-Kalām*, 1:43.

According to non-muqallids, reciting *Sūrat al-Fātiḥah* behind the imām is necessary (*wājib*), whilst recitation of any other *sūrah*, other than *Sūrat al-Fātiḥah*, is prohibited.

The non-muqallids do not have any evidence for this differentiation in the ruling, as Mawlānā Muḥammad Ismāʿīl Salafī said: "There is no clear ruling which negates reciting anything apart from *Surat al-Fātiḥah*. However, there is some doubt regarding this from the ḥadīth of Sayyidunā ʿUbādah ﷺ. However, the reality is that the purpose of his narration is to only demonstrate the obligation of *Surat al-Fātiḥah*; it is not to negate any further recitation."[151]

❧

Ḥadīth 17

THE RECITATION OF THE IMĀM IS SUFFICIENT FOR THE FOLLOWER

The other reason why it is prohibited for the follower (*muqtadī*) to recite behind the imām is due to the recitation of the imām sufficing the follower (*muqtadī*). Therefore, there is no need for the follower (*muqtadī*) to recite anything, and this is what Rasūlullāh ﷺ taught.

Sayyidunā Jābir ﷺ said that Rasūlullāh ﷺ said:

مَنْ كَانَ لَهُ إِمَامٌ فَقِرَاءَةُ الْإِمَامِ لَهُ قِرَاءَةٌ.

Whoever has an imām, the imām's recitation is recitation for him (i.e., the follower).[152]

151 *Rasūl-i-Akram* ﷺ *Kī Namāz*, p. 77.

152 *Musnad al-Imām Abī Ḥanīfah* through Abū Nuʿaym's narration (228); *Muwaṭṭā Imām Muḥammad*, p. 198; *Sharḥ Maʿānī al-Āthār*, 1:149; *Musnad Aḥmad ibn Manīʿ*; *Musnad ʿAbd ibn Ḥumayd*, quoted from *Itḥāf al-Khiyarat al-Maharah*, 2:216.

Imām Aḥmad ibn Abū Bakr al-Būṣīrī (d. 840 AH) said after quoting the aforementioned ḥadīth from *Musnad Aḥmad ibn Manī`* and *Musnad ʿAbd ibn Ḥumayd,* with its chain: "The first chain of the ḥadīth of Jābir[153] is authentic according to the criteria of the two Shaykhs (Bukhārī and Muslim) and the second chain[154] is according to the criteria of Muslim."[155]

Shaykh al-Albānī has written: "Shaykh al-Islām Ibn Taymiyyah declared it strong, as mentioned in *al-Furūʿ* of Ibn ʿAbd al-Hādī (2:48), and al-Būṣīrī has authenticated some of its chains."[156]

Contrary to the aforementioned ḥadīth, and other authentic ḥadīths, there is no authentic ḥadīth that affirms reciting *Surat al-Fātiḥah* behind the imām. Even the main proof, i.e., the ḥadīth of Sayyidunā ʿUbādah ibn Ṣāmit , that is presented to support reciting *Surat al-Fātiḥah* behind the imām, is weak according to Shaykh al-Albānī himself.

If we suppose this ḥadīth to be authentic, the obligation of reciting *Surat al-Fātiḥah* can still not be deduced from it, as stated by Shaykh al-Albānī.[157]

❧

Ḥadīth 18
IT IS *SUNNAH* TO SAY *ĀMĪN* QUIETLY

After the imām finishes reciting *Sūrat al-Fātiḥah*, it is *sunnah* for the imām and follower (*muqtadī*) to say *āmīn* quietly.

153 *Musnad Aḥmad ibn Manī`*

154 *Musnad ʿAbd ibn Ḥumayd*

155 *Itḥāf al-Khiyarat al-Maharah*, 2:216.

156 *Ṣifat Salāt al-Nabīyy* ﷺ, p. 100.

157 *Mishkāt al-Maṣābīḥ*, ed. Nāṣir al-Dīn al-Albānī, 1:270.

Sayyidunā Wā'il ibn Ḥujr ؓ narrates:

أَنَّهُ صَلَّى مَعَ النَّبِيِّ ﷺ حِيْنَ قَالَ: غَيْرِالْمَغْضُوْبِ عَلَيْهِمْ وَلَاالضَّالِّيْنَ: قَالَ آمِيْنَ، يَخْفِضُ بِهَا صَوْتَهُ. وَفِيْ رِوَايَةٍ: أَخْفَى بِهَا صَوْتَهُ.

He (i.e., Sayyidunā Wā'il ibn Ḥujr ؓ) performed ṣalāh with Nabī ﷺ. After he ﷺ said: غَيْرِالْمَغْضُوْبِ عَلَيْهِمْ وَلَاالضَّالِّين he said *āmīn*, whilst lowering his voice.[158] In another narration: He ﷺ said *āmīn* quietly.[159]

Imām al-Ḥākim (d. 405 AH) and Imām al-Dhahabī (d. 748 AH) conclude regarding the aforementioned ḥadīth that it is authentic upon the criteria of the two Shaykhs (Imām al-Bukhārī and Imām Muslim).[160] ʿAllāmah al-Shawkānī (d. 1255 AH) also authenticated this ḥadīth, and regarded the objection made on its authenticity by Imām al-Bukhārī and others to be insignificant.[161]

Mawlānā Nawāb Nūr al-Ḥasan Khān (d. 1336 AH) has acknowledged that the ḥadīths on saying *āmīn* quietly in ṣalāh are authentic.[162]

This ḥadīth is supported by several other ḥadīths. In ḥadīth sixteen, the follower (*muqtadī*) is instructed to say *āmīn* after the imām reads: غَيْرِالْمَغْضُوْبِ عَلَيْهِمْ وَلَاالضَّالِّين

This is clear evidence that it is not *sunnah* for the imām to say *āmīn* loudly, because if it was a *sunnah* for the imām to say *āmīn* loudly (like *Surat al-Fātiḥah*), Rasūlullāh ﷺ would have instructed to say *āmīn* when the imām says *āmīn*. Also, it is stated further in the same ḥadīth that when the imām says:

158 *Mustadrak al-Ḥākim* (2913).

159 *Dāraquṭnī* (1256).

160 *Mustadrak al-Ḥākim*, 2:253.

161 *Nayl al-Awṭār*, 1:386.

162 *ʿArf al-Jādī*, p. 29-30.

Sami' allāhu li man ḥamidah, the follower should say: *Allāhumma rabbanā laka 'l-ḥamd*. It is apparent that the words: *Allāhumma rabbanā laka 'l-ḥamd* are said quietly. A similar instruction has been narrated regarding *āmīn*. Therefore, both the imām and the followers should say *āmīn* quietly.

Furthermore, it is reported that Sayyidunā ʿUmar ﵁ and Sayyidunā ʿAlī ﵁, and the jurist Ṣaḥābī, Sayyidunā ʿAbdullāh ibn Masʿūd ﵁ would say *āmīn* quietly in ṣalāh.[163] This report is authentic, and its narrator, Abū Saʿd al-Baqqāl, is reliable.[164]

Alongside these three, the majority of the Ṣaḥābah and Tābiʿūn would say *āmīn* quietly.

The great hadith scholar (*muḥaddith*) and famous jurist, Imām Muḥammad ibn Jarīr al-Ṭabarī (d. 310 AH) gave preference to saying *āmīn* quietly. He said:

وَإِنْ كُنْتُ مُخْتَارًا خَفْضَ الصَّوْتِ بِهَا، إِذْ كَانَ أَكْثَرُ الصَّحَابَةِ وَالتَّابِعِيْنَ عَلَى ذٰلِكَ.

I prefer saying *āmīn* quietly in ṣalāh, as this was the practice of the majority of the Ṣaḥābah and Tābiʿūn.[165]

Mawlānā Nadhīr Ḥusain al-Dihlawī* acknowledged it is better to say *āmīn* quietly in ṣalāh.[166] Similarly, ʿAllāmah Waḥīd al-Zamān stated: "This issue was disputed amongst the Ṣaḥābah and Tābiʿūn. Some of them would say *āmīn* loudly, whilst others would say it quietly."[167] It should be noted that according to those who prefer saying *āmīn* loudly, this only applies to the imām; it will be *sunnah* for the followers to say it quietly.

Shaykh al-Albānī wrote:

نَصَّ الشَّافِعِيُّ عَلَى أَنَّ الْإِمَامَ يَجْهَرُ بِآمِيْنَ دُوْنَ مُقْتَدِيِيْنَ، وَهَذَا هُوَ الصَّوَابُ.

163 *Sharḥ Maʿānī al-Āthār*, 1:140, *al-Muʿjam al-Kabīr* (2347).

164 See Mawlānā Zahoor's: *Rakʿāt Tarāwīḥ Ayk Taḥqīqī Jā'izah*, p. 169-172.

165 *Al-Jawhar al-Naqiyy*, 2:58.

166 *Fatāwā Nadhīriyyah*, 1:448.

167 *Lughāt al-Ḥadīth*, p. 115.

Imām al-Shāfiʿī stated that the imām will say *āmīn* loudly and not the followers, and this is the correct opinion.[168]

❧

Ḥadīth 19
IT IS *SUNNAH* NOT TO RAISE THE HANDS EXCEPT WITH THE OPENING *TAKBĪR*

Once a person completes the recitation (*qirā'ah*), he will go into *rukūʿ* without raising the hands. Similarly, when rising from *rukūʿ*, and when standing up for the third *rakʿah*, one will not raise the hands. Rasūlullāh ﷺ would only raise his hands in the opening takbir (*takbīr taḥrīmah*). ʿAlqamah ﷺ reports that Sayyidunā ʿAbdullāh ibn Masʿūd ﷺ said:

أَلَا أُصَلِّيْ بِكُمْ صَلَاةَ رَسُوْلِ اللهِ؟ فَصَلَّى، فَلَمْ يَرْفَعْ يَدَيْهِ إِلَّا فِيْ أَوَّلِ مَرَّةٍ.

"Shall I not lead you in ṣalāh as Rasūlullāh ﷺ prayed?" He then prayed ṣalāh, and only raised his hands in the beginning.[169]

Imām al-Tirmidhī graded this ḥadīth as sound (*ḥasan*). In some of the manuscripts of Tirmidhī, the grading of this ḥadīth has come with the words: sound and authentic.[170]

ʿAllāmah Ibn al-Turkumānī (d. 745 AH) said all the narrators of this ḥadīth are upon the criteria of Imām Muslim.[171] Imām al-Dāraquṭnī (d. 385 AH), Imām Ibn al-Qaṭṭān (d. 628 AH) and others deemed this ḥadīth authentic.[172]

ʿAllāmah Aḥmad Shākir said:

168 *Al-Ḥāwī min Fatāwā al-Shaykh al-Albānī*, p. 222.
169 *Tirmidhī* (257); *Abū Dāwūd* (746); *Nasā'ī* (1060).
170 *Tirmidhī*, ed. of Aḥmad Shākir, 2:41
171 *Al-Jawhar al-Naqiyy*, 2:78.
172 *Kitāb al-ʿIlal*, 2:382; *al-La'ālī al-Maṣnūʿah*, 2:18.

هَذَا الْحَدِيْثُ صَحَّحَهُ ابْنُ حَزْمٍ وَغَيْرُهُ مِنَ الْحُفَّاظِ، وَهُوَ حَدِيْثٌ صَحِيْحٌ، وَمَا قَالُوْا فِى تَعْلِيْلِهِ لَيْسَ بِعِلَّةٍ.

This ḥadīth has been authenticated by Ibn Ḥazm (in *al-Muḥallā*, 3:140) and other ḥadīth scholars, and it is an authentic ḥadīth. Whatever they said to fault it is not really a fault.[173]

Shaykh Nāsir al-Dīn Albānī has written:

وَالْحَقُّ أَنَّهُ حَدِيْثٌ صَحِيْحٌ ، وَإِسْنَادُهُ صَحِيْحٌ عَلَى شَرْطِ مُسْلِمٍ ، وَلَمْ نَجِدْ لِمَنْ أَعَلَّهُ حُجَّةً يَصْلُحُ التَّعَلُّقُ بِهَا وَرَدُّ الْحَدِيْثُ مِنْ أَجْلِهَا.

The truth is that it is an authentic ḥadīth, and its chain is authentic according to the criteria of Muslim. We did not find for those who weakened it any such proof that is worthy of holding onto and due to which the ḥadīth can be refuted.[174]

Mawlānā ʿAṭā'ullāh Ḥanīf* also acknowledged this ḥadīth to be authentic.[175]

Some non-muqallids accused the narrator of this ḥadīth, Sufyān al-Thawrī, of *tadlīs*, whereas Imām al-Dāraquṭnī rejected this allegation and said that Thawrī heard this ḥadīth from his teacher (ʿĀsim ibn Kulayb).[176] Furthermore, the senior non-muqallid scholars clearly stated that according to the ḥadīth scholars (*muḥaddithūn*), Sufyān al-Thawrī's *tadlīs* is not harmful,[177]

173 *Tirmidhī*, ed. of Aḥmad Shākir, 2:41.

174 *Mishkāt al-Maṣābīḥ*, ed. Nāṣir al-Dīn al-Albānī, 1:254.

175 *Al-Taʿlīqāt al-Salafiyyah*, 2:107.

176 *Kitāb al-ʿIlal* (804).

177 *Iḥkām al-Aḥkām*, 1:137; *Maqālāt Mubārakpūrī*, p. 368; *Ibkār al-Minan*, p. 198; *Maqālāt Rāshidiyyah*, 1:305-347, 3:490; *Khayr al-Kalām*, p. 214.

especially when this ḥadīth is strengthened by many raised (*marfūʿ*) narrations.[178]

Also, it is established from authentic ḥadīths that many Ṣaḥābah, including Sayyidunā Abū Bakr, Sayyidunā ʿUmar and Sayyidunā ʿAlī ﷺ would only raise their hands with the *takbīr taḥrīmah*.[179]

Mawlānā Nadhīr Ḥusayn al-Dihlawi (d. 1340 AH) said: "It is clear to the scholars of truth that arguing and fighting over raising the hands when going into *rukūʿ* and rising therefrom is not free from prejudice and ignorance. This is because at various times, both types of actions, i.e., raising the hands and not raising them, are established and there is evidence on both sides."[180]

ʿAllāmah Ibn Ḥazm al-Ẓāhirī (d. 456 AH) said:

وَإِنْ لَّمْ نَرْفَعْ فَقَدْ صَلَّيْنَا كَمَا كَانَ عَلَيْهِ السَّلَامُ يُصَلِّيْ.

If we do not raise our hands (besides the *takbīr taḥrīmah*), we have nonetheless prayed like he ﷺ would pray.[181]

Mawlānā Thanā'ullāh Amritsarī* (d. 1948 AH) said: "Our (non-muqallid) stance is that not raising the hands will not affect the validity of ṣalāh."[182]

Some contemporary non-muqallids exaggerated in this issue, to the extent that they deemed these two issues to be imperative and compulsory, whereas their reputable scholar,

178 *Muslim* (899); *Ṣaḥīh Abī ʿAwānah* (1251); *Musnad al-Ḥumaydī* (614); *Abū Yaʿlā* (1685, 1688, 5017); Abū Nuʿaym's *Musnad al-Imām Abī Ḥanīfah*, p. 156. Ironically, the same non-muqallids have no issue using Sufyān al-Thawrī's ḥadīth to prove saying *āmīn* loudly and no mention is made of his *tadlīs* in that case, even though it opposes the ḥadīth of a great non-*mudallis* like Shuʿbah.

179 *Naṣb al-Rāyah*, 1:405-406; *al-Dirāyah*, 1:153.

180 *Fatāwā Nadhīriyyah*, 1:441.

181 *Al-Muḥallā*, 3:140.

182 *Fatāwā Thanā'iyyah*, 1:362; *Fatāwā ʿUlamā'-i-Ḥadīth*, 3:154.

Allāmah Waḥīd al-Zamān (d. 1338 AH) clearly stated: "If a person regards the issues of raising the hands (*rafʿ al-yadayn*) and saying *āmīn* loudly (*āmīn bi 'l-jahr*) to be compulsory and imperative, and censures the one who does not act upon them, this person is misguided and the satan has overpowered him."[183]

None of the ḥadīths used by non-muqallids as evidence can clearly establish their claim. Even their most substantial proof, namely the ḥadīth of Sayyidunā Ibn ʿUmar ﵄ (which reports raising of the hands when going into and rising from *rukūʿ*) is not free from confusion (*iḍṭirāb*).

This is perhaps the reason why Imām Mālik ﵀, the foremost narrator of this ḥadīth, took out the last portion of this ḥadīth (which mentions raising of the hands when rising from *rukūʿ*) from the final manuscript of his *Muwaṭṭa'*, according to the transmission of Yaḥyā al-Laythī. This ḥadīth is narrated in its entirety in the old manuscripts of the book. Many ḥadīth scholars (*muḥaddithūn*) have clearly stated that Imām Mālik purposefully took out those ḥadīths which can be found in the old manuscripts of *Muwaṭṭa'* but not in the final manuscript of Yaḥyā al-Laythī, as he was not content with their authenticity.[184]

Imām al-Dāraquṭnī (d. 385 AH) said regarding this ḥadīth of Sayyidunā Ibn ʿUmar ﵄:

وَأَحْسَبُ أَنَّ مَالِكًا لَمْ يَذْكُرْ هَذَا اللَّفْظَ فِي مُوَطَّئِهِ، وَقَصَّرَ عَنْهُ، لِأَنَّ مَذْهَبَهُ كَانَ لَا يُرْفَعُ يَدَيْهِ لِلرُّكُوعِ، وَلَا يُرْفَعُ إِلَّا فِي التَّكْبِيرَةِ الْأُولَى.

> I think Mālik did not mention this wording in his *Muwaṭṭa'* and removed it, as his opinion was the hands should not be raised for *rukūʿ*, but rather only be raised for the *takbīr taḥrīmah*.[185]

183 *Lughāt al-Hadīth*, 1:62.

184 *Al-Tamhīd*, 9:214; Dāraquṭnī's *al-ʿIlal*, 5:238.

185 *Al-ʿIlal* (2993).

In addition to the above, the main narrator of this primary proof, Sayyidunā ʿAbdullāh ibn ʿUmar ؓ would not raise his hands except with the *takbīr taḥrīmah.*[186] Likewise, the second primary proof of non-muqallids is the narration of Sayyidunā Mālik ibn al-Ḥuwayrith ؓ, in which some transmissions (*ṭuruq*) report raising of the hands between the *sajdahs*, whereas non-muqallids do not practice this.[187] Therefore, apart from the time of *takbīr taḥrīmah*, not raising the hands is preferable.

Ḥadīth 20
THE *SUNNAH* METHOD OF *RUKŪʿ*, *QAWMAH*, *SAJDAH* AND *JALSAH*

The *sunnah* method of *rukūʿ*, *qawmah* (standing up from *rukūʿ*), *sajdah* and *jalsah* (sitting between the two *sajdahs*), which has been explained in this ḥadīth reported by Sālim al-Barrād:

أَتَيْنَا عُقْبَةَ بْنَ عَمْرٍو الْأَنْصَارِيَّ أَبَا مَسْعُوْدٍ ؓ فَقُلْنَا لَهُ: حَدِّثْنَا عَنْ صَلٰوةِ رَسُوْلِ اللهِ ، فَقَامَ بَيْنَ أَيْدِيْنَا فِي الْمَسْجِدِ فَكَبَّرَ، فَلَمَّا رَكَعَ وَضَعَ يَدَيْهِ عَلَى رُكْبَتَيْهِ، وَجَعَلَ أَصَابِعَهُ أَسْفَلَ مِنْ ذٰلِكَ، وَجَافٰى بَيْنَ مِرْفَقَيْهِ حَتّٰى اسْتَقَرَّ كُلُّ شَيْءٍ مِّنْهُ، ثُمَّ قَالَ: سَمِعَ اللهُ لِمَنْ حَمِدَهُ، فَقَامَ حَتّٰى اسْتَقَرَّ كُلُّ شَيْءٍ مِّنْهُ، ثُمَّ كَبَّرَ وَسَجَدَ وَوَضَعَ كَفَّيْهِ عَلَى الْأَرْضِ، ثُمَّ جَافٰى بَيْنَ مِرْفَقَيْهِ حَتّٰى اسْتَقَرَّ كُلُّ شَيْءٍ مِّنْهُ، ثُمَّ رَفَعَ رَأْسَهُ، فَجَلَسَ حَتّٰى اسْتَقَرَّ كُلُّ شَيْءٍ مِّنْهُ، فَفَعَلَ مِثْلَ ذٰلِكَ أَيْضًا، ثُمَّ صَلّٰى أَرْبَعَ رَكَعَاتٍ مِثْلَ هٰذِهِ الرَّكْعَةِ، فَصَلّٰى صَلَاتَهُ ثُمَّ قَالَ: هٰكَذَا رَأَيْنَا رَسُوْلَ اللهِ يُصَلِّيْ.

186 *Muṣannaf Ibn Abī Shaybah*, 1:268; *Kitāb al-Ḥujjah ʿalā Ahl al-Madīnah*, 1:97.
187 *Nasāʾī* (1087, 1088).

> We came to ʿUqbah ibn ʿAmr al-Anṣārī Abū Masʿūd ﷺ and said to him: 'Tell us about the ṣalāh of Rasūlullāh ﷺ.' He stood up before us in the mosque and said the *takbīr*. When he bowed, he placed his hands upon his knees and put his fingers further down, and kept his elbows away from his sides, until every part of him settled. Then he said: *Samiʿ allāhu li man ḥamidah.* He then stood until every part of him settled. Thereafter, he said the *takbīr* and prostrated, putting his palms on the ground, and he kept his elbows away from his sides, until every part of him settled. He then raised his head and sat, until every part of him settled. He then repeated this. Thereafter, he performed four *rakʿahs* of ṣalāh in the same way as this *rakʿah*, and completed his ṣalāh. He then said: 'This is how we saw Rasūlullāh ﷺ perform ṣalāh.'[188]

Imām al-Ḥākim (d. 405 AH) and Imām al-Dhahabī (d. 748 AH) said this is a ḥadīth with an authentic chain.[189]

❧

Ḥadīth 21
THE *SUNNAH* METHOD OF *SAJDAH*

The *sunnah* method of performing *sajdah* is that when one proceeds for *sajdah*, they should first place their knees on the ground and then their hands, and when rising from *sajdah*, they will do the opposite, i.e., first lift the hands from the ground and then the knees.

Sayyidunā Wā'il ibn Ḥujr ﷺ said:

---

188 *Abū Dāwūd* (863); *Nasā'ī* (1039); *Mustadrak al-Ḥākim* (816).

189 *Mustadrak al-Ḥākim*, 1:347.

رَأَيْتُ النَّبِيَّ ﷺ إِذَا سَجَدَ وَضَعَ رُكْبَتَيْهِ قَبْلَ يَدَيْهِ، وَإِذَا نَهَضَ رَفَعَ يَدَيْهِ قَبْلَ رُكْبَتَيْهِ.

I saw Nabī ﷺ place his knees (on the ground) before his hands when proceeding for *sajdah*, and when standing from *sajdah*, raise his hands before his knees.[190]

Imām al-Tirmidhī (d. 279 AH) said this ḥadīth is sound (*ḥasan*), and Imām al-Ḥākim (d. 405 AH) and Imām al-Dhahabī (d. 748 AH) classed this ḥadīth to be on the criteria of Imām Muslim.[191]

Imām Ibn Khuzaymah (d. 311 AH) narrates this ḥadīth in his *Ṣaḥīḥ* compilation, and he said that the ḥadīth which states placing the knees before the hands when going into *sajdah* is abrogated (*mansūkh*). To support this abrogation, Imām Ibn Khuzaymah narrates the ḥadīth of Sayyidunā Saʿd ؓ in which he says that we used to place our hands before our knees, whereafter we were instructed to place our knees on the ground before placing our hands.[192]

Imām Ibn al-Mundhir (d. 318 AH) deemed this ḥadīth to be established (*thābit*) and preferred (*rājiḥ*).[193] Imām al-Baghawī (d. 516 AH) also deemed it preferred (*rājiḥ*).[194]

In addition to this, Imām Ibn Ḥibbān (d. 354 AH) narrated this ḥadīth in his *Ṣaḥīḥ* compilation.[195] Therefore, accusing the narrator of this ḥadīth, Sharīk, of committing *tadlīs* is incorrect. Mawlānā ʿAbd al-Ra'ūf and Mawlānā Irshād al-Ḥaqq al-Atharī said that according to what Ibn Ḥibbān ؒ stated in

190 *Abū Dāwūd* (837); *Tirmidhī* (268); *Mustadrak al-Ḥākim* (822).

191 *Mustadrak al-Ḥākim*, 1:349.

192 *Ibn Khuzaymah* (628, 629).

193 *Al-Awsaṭ*, 3:328.

194 *Maṣābīḥ al-Sunnah*, 1:113.

195 *Al-Iḥsān bi-Tartīb Ṣaḥīḥ Ibn Ḥibbān* (1908).

the introduction to his *Ṣaḥīḥ*[196] regarding those who do *tadlīs*, even if the narrators do not clearly state they directly narrated or heard, it will be understood as having been heard directly nonetheless.[197]

Therefore, when Imām Ibn Ḥibbān narrates the ḥadīth of Sharīk in his *Ṣaḥīḥ*, this in itself is evidence that Sharīk's narration is through directly narrating or hearing. Hence, objecting to the aforementioned ḥadīth because of Sharīk is futile.

Furthermore, Mawlānā ʿAbd al-Raḥmān Mubarakpūrī has quoted that Imām al-Ḥalabī included Sharīk amongst those scholars whose *tadlīs* is not harmful.[198] Also, this ḥadīth of Sayyidunā Wā'il ibn Ḥujr ﷺ (from the narration of ʿAbd al-Jabbār ibn Wā'il) is supported by the narrations of Sayyidunā Saʿd ﷺ and Sayyidunā Anas ﷺ.[199]

Mawlānā Muḥammad Ṣādiq Siyālkawtī* said after narrating the aforementioned ḥadīth, "It is understood that one should place their knees before their hands when proceeding from *sajdah* to *sajdah*. The majority of the imāms, of the Ḥanafī, Shāfiʿī and Ḥanbalī school, act upon this ḥadīth. It is also stated in *Ṣaḥīḥ Ibn Khuzaymah* that when performing *sajdah*, Rasūlullāh ﷺ would first put his knees down."[200]

Also, Mawlānā Muḥammad Ṣādiq Siyālkawtī, whilst giving preference to the narration of Sayyidunā Wā'il ibn Ḥujr ﷺ over the narration of Sayyidunā Abū Hurayrah ﷺ (which mentions one should place the hands before the knees when going into *sajdah*) said: "In short, preference will be given to the first ḥadīth. Abū Sulaymān al-Khaṭṭābī said the ḥadīth of Wā'il ibn

---

196 1:161-162.

197 *Al-Qawl al-Maqbūl*, p. 394, *Tawḍīḥ al-Kalām*, 1:238.

198 *Maqālāt Mubārakpūrī*, p. 368.

199 *Abū Dāwūd* (839); *Al-Muʿjam al-Awsaṭ* (5911); *Ibn Khuzaymah* (628); *Mustadrak al-Ḥākim* (822).

200 *Ṣalāt al-Rasūl*, p. 244.

Ḥujr is more authentic than this ḥadīth. Thus, the predominant practice is on the ḥadīth of Wā'il ibn Ḥujr."[201]

Shaykh Muḥammad ibn ʿAbd al-Wahhāb writes: "When Rasūlullāh ﷺ would go into *sajdah*, he would first place his knees on the ground, then his hands, and then his forehead and nose. This is the correct method, because he ﷺ would first place that limb which was the closest to the ground, followed by the next closest limb. When he ﷺ would rise from *sajdah*, he would do the opposite, i.e., lift the body part which was the highest, and then the next highest. Thus, he would raise his head, then his hands and then his knees."[202]

ʿAllāmāh Waḥīd al-Zamān was also of this opinion.[203] In addition to the above, Mawlānā Muḥammad Ibrāhīm Siyālkawtī has given preference to the aforementioned opinion, and the wisdom he stated for this opinion is that when going into *sajdah*, the sequence of placing the body parts on the ground is correct, and the forehead and nose come between the hands.[204]

❧

Ḥadīth 22

THE *SUNNAH* METHOD OF *SAJDAH* FOR WOMEN

Amongst the positions in which a woman's ṣalāh differs from a man's is *sajdah*. A man will keep his body away from the ground and his elbows away from his body, as mentioned in ḥadīth twenty. However, a woman will keep parts

201 *Salāt al-Rasūl*, p. 245.

202 *Mu'allafāt al-Shaykh Muḥammad ibn ʿAbd al-Wahhāb*, 1:15.

203 *Nuzul al-Abrār*, 1:80.

204 *Ṣalāt al-Nabiyy*, p.39.

of her body on the ground during *sajdah*, whilst keeping her stomach close to her thighs.

Sayyidunā Yazīd ibn Abī Ḥabīb ﷺ narrates:

أَنَّ رَسُوْلَ اللهِ ﷺ مَرَّ عَلَى امْرَأَتَيْنِ تُصَلِّيَانِ، فَقَالَ إِذَاسَجَدْتُمَا فَضُمَّا بَعْضَ اللَّحْمِ إِلَى الْأَرْضِ، فَإِنَّ الْمَرْأَةَ لَيْسَتْ فِي ذَلِكَ كَالرَّجُلِ.

Rasūlullāh ﷺ passed by two women who were praying ṣalāh. He ﷺ said, "When you perform *sajdah*, then keep part of the body on the ground, because a woman is not like a man in this regard."[205]

The chain of transmission of this ḥadīth is completely authentic, albeit it is a *mursal* narration, because Yazīd ibn Abī Ḥabīb who narrates the ḥadīth from Rasūlullāh ﷺ is not a Ṣaḥābī, but rather a Tābiʿī. A narration in which a Tābiʿī reports directly from Rasūlullāh ﷺ, without the link of a Ṣaḥābī, is known as *mursal.*

According to most scholars, such as Imām Abū Ḥanīfah, Imām Mālik, Imām Aḥmad, Imām al-Thawrī ﷺ and others, a *mursal* narration is evidential without any additional condition.

Imām Shāfiʿī ﷺ and other ḥadīth scholars only deem a supported (*muʿtaḍad) mursal* to be evidence. A supported *mursal* is a narration which is supported by another, even though the supporting narration may be weak.[206]

Mawlānā ʿAbd al-Raḥmān Mubārakpūrī wrote that a supported *mursal* is evidential by consensus,[207] and supported *mursal* narrations can definitely be used as evidence .[208]

205 *Marāsīl Abī Dāwūd* (89).

206 Ibn Ḥajar's *al-Nukat ʿalā Kitāb Ibn al-Ṣalāḥ*, p. 214; *Fatḥ al-Mughīth*, 1:164; *Ḥujjatullāh al-Bālighah*, 1:140; *Sharḥ al-Zarqānī ʿalā al-Manẓūmah al-Bayqūniyyah*, p. 56.

207 *Ibkār al-Minan*, p. 143.

208 *Taḥqīq al-Kalām*, 1:95.

The aforementioned ḥadīth is also a supported *mursal* narration, thus substantial as evidence according to all, because it is supported by several other narrations.

We present the translation of two narrations thereof as an example:

1. Sayyidunā Ibn ʿUmar ﷺ narrates that Rasūlullāh ﷺ said, "When a woman performs *sajdah*, she should press her stomach against her thighs in a manner which is most concealing for her."[209]

2. Sayyidunā Abū Saʿīd al-Khudrī ﷺ narrates that Rasūlullāh ﷺ taught women to press themselves (against the ground) in *sajdah*.[210]

In addition to this, the narrations of Sayyidunā ʿAlī ﷺ, Sayyidunā ʿAbdullāh ibn ʿAbbās ﷺ and others further support this ḥadīth.[211]

According to senior non-muqallid scholars also, the ruling of *sajdah* for a woman is different to that of a man. ʿAllāmah Amīr al-Ṣanʿānī (d. 1182 AH) writes under the ḥadīth of *Ṣaḥīḥ Muslim* which instructs one to keep the elbows away from the body during *sajdah*:

وَ هَذَا فِيْ حَقِّ الرَّجُلِ، لَا الْمَرْأَةِ، فَإِنَّهَا تُخَالِفُهُ فِيْ ذَلِكَ.

This ruling is for men, not women, as she will oppose him in that regard.

Thereafter, he cites the *mursal* narration of Yazīd ibn Abī Ḥabīb as evidence.[212]

Mawlānā ʿAbd al-Jabbār Ghaznawī (d. 1923 AH) has also

209 *Al-Sunan al-Kubrā*, 2:223; *Tarīkh Aṣbahān*, 1:200.

210 Ibid.

211 Ibid, *Muṣannaf Ibn Abī Shaybah*, 1:302.

212 *Subul al-Salām*, 1:192.

cited the narrations of Yazīd ibn Abī Ḥabīb and others, whereafter he writes: "This is the constant practice (*taʿāmul*) of the Ahl al-Sunnah and the four schools."

He further cites references from the reliable books of the four schools, and then writes: "The joining (*inḍimām*) and lowering (*inkhifāḍ*) (i.e., to join the body with the thighs and to lower the body towards the ground in *sajdah*) of women is established from ḥadīths, and it is the practice of the vast majority of scholars from the four schools and others. One who refuses this is ignorant of the books of ḥadīth and the practice of the people of knowledge."[213]

Mawlānā ʿAbdullāh Rawparī (d. 1384 AH) also acknowledged that the method of *sajdah* for women is different to that of men. He writes: "However, there are is an exception for women in some ḥadīths, i.e., a woman (in *sajdah*) will not raise her back, but rather she will join it with her thighs. Although there are some weaknesses in these narrations, they have supporting narrations (*mu'ayyidāt*), and can be acted upon."[214] ʿAllāmah Waḥīd al-Zamān (d. 1337 AH) was also of the same opinion.[215]

❧

Ḥadīth 23
IT IS NOT *SUNNAH* TO SIT TO REST BETWEEN THE SECOND *SAJDAH* AND STANDING

In every *rakʿah*, two *sajdahs* are obligatory; on completion of two *sajdahs*, one *rakʿah* will be complete. After completing the first *rakʿah*, one should immediately stand up for the second

213 *Fatāwā ʿUlamā'-i-Ḥadīth*, 3:149.
214 *Fatāwā Ahl-i-Ḥadīth*, 1:523.
215 *Kanz al-Ḥaqā'iq*, p. 22; *Nuzul al-Abrār*, 1:85.

rakʿah without any pause, as is it not *sunnah* to sit (known as *jalsah istirāḥah*, the rest-sitting) between the second *sajdah* and *qiyām*.

Sayyidunā Abū Hurayrah ؓ and Sayyidunā Rifāʿah ibn Rāfiʿ ؓ narrate that Rasūlullāh ﷺ said to a Bedouin, whom he ﷺ was teaching the method of ṣalāh:

إِذَا قُمْتَ إِلَى الصَّلَوةِ فَأَسْبِغِ الْوُضُوْءَ، ثُمَّ اسْتَقْبِلِ الْقِبْلَةَ، فَكَبِّرْ وَاقْرَأْ بِمَا تَيَسَّرَ مَعَكَ مِنَ الْقُرْآنِ، ثُمَّ ارْكَعْ حَتَّى تَطْمَئِنَّ رَاكِعًا، ثُمَّ ارْفَعْ رَأْسَكَ حَتَّى تَعْتَدِلَ قَائِمًا، ثُمَّ اسْجُدْ حَتَّى تَطْمَئِنَّ سَاجِدًا، ثُمَّ ارْفَعْ حَتَّى تَسْتَوِيَ وَتَطْمَئِنَّ جَالِسًا، ثُمَّ اسْجُدْ حَتَّى تَطْمَئِنَّ سَاجِدًا، ثُمَّ ارْفَعْ حَتَّى تَسْتَوِيَ قَائِمًا ، ثُمَّ افْعَلْ ذَلِكَ فِي صَلَوتِكَ كُلِّهَا.

When you stand for ṣalāh, perform the ablution properly, face the *qiblah* and say the *takbīr* (*Allāhu akbar*). Then (after *Ṣurat al-Fātiḥah*) recite of the Qur'ān what is easy for you. Then bow, and remain in this state till you feel at rest in bowing. Then raise your head and stand straight. Then prostrate till you feel at rest in prostration, then sit up till you feel at rest while sitting, and then prostrate again till you feel at rest in prostration. Then raise your head and stand straight, and do all this in all of your ṣalāh. [216]

216 *Bukhārī* (6251, 6667); *Aḥmad* (19206). In some transmissions of this ḥadīth, which are narrated by Sayyidunā Abū Hurayrah ؓ, instead of the words حَتَّى تَسْتَوِيَ قَائِمًا, the words حَتَّى تَسْتَوِيَ جَالِسًا (until you sit straight) have been reported which are irregular (*shādh*). Therefore, Mawlānā ʿAbd al-Ra'ūf has written: "This (i.e. the narration with the words حَتَّى تَسْتَوِيَ قَائِمًا) is the authentic narration, as stated by Imām al-Bayhaqī and Ḥāfiẓ Ibn Ḥajar in his *Talkhīṣ* (1:255). Moreover, the words: ثُمَّ ارْفَعْ حَتَّى تَطْمَئِنَّ جَالِسًا are irregular, and Imām al-Bukhārī has indicated towards their irregularity. Refer to *Fatḥ al-Bārī*, 2:279, 11:37." (*al-Qawl al-Maqbūl*, p. 53). Also, Ḥāfiẓ Ibn Rajab deemed the words حَتَّى تَسْتَوِيَ قَائِمًا to be correct and the words حَتَّى تَسْتَوِيَ جَالِسًا to be incorrect and unpreserved (Ibn Rajab's *Fatḥ al-Bārī*).

This is a verbal (*qawlī*) ḥadīth, which is stronger than a ḥadīth of action (*fi'lī*), and it is a very authentic narration. In this ḥadīth, the Messenger of Allāh ﷺ instructed the Ṣaḥābī to stand up immediately after the second *sajdah*. If the *jalsah istirāḥah* was a *sunnah* at this point, Rasūlullāh ﷺ would have instructed him to sit after performing the second *sajdah*, instead of standing up immediately. It is thus clear that the *jalsah istirāḥah* is not *sunnah*.

Ḥāfiẓ Ibn Rajab (d. 795 AH) mentioned the opinion of Imām Aḥmad ibn Ḥanbal رحمه الله under this ḥadīth, saying:

وَاسْتَدَلَّ بِهِ عَلَى أَنَّهُ لَا يُجْلَسُ قَبْلَ قِيَامِهِ.

Imām Aḥmad used this ḥadīth as evidence for not sitting before standing up.[217]

Imām Ibn 'Abd al-Barr رحمه الله (d. 463 AH) has also used this ḥadīth as evidence against *jalsah istirāḥah*.[218] Furthermore, this ḥadīth is supported by numerous other ḥadīths, one of them being the ḥadīth of Sayyidunā Abū Ḥumayd al-Sā'idī رضي الله عنه (that the non-muqallids themselves use as evidence in the issue of raising the hands), wherein he described the method of Rasūlullāh's ﷺ *sajdah* and how he would rise from it as follows:

ثُمَّ كَبَّرَ فَسَجَدَ، ثُمَّ كَبَّرَ فَقَامَ وَلَمْ يَتَوَرَّكْ.

Then, he said the *takbīr* and performed *sajdah*. Then, he said the *takbīr* and stood up, and he did not sit.[219]

Ḥāfiẓ Ibn Rajab (d. 795 AH) says under this ḥadīth:

وَ هَذِهِ الرِّوَايَةُ صَرِيحَةٌ فِي أَنَّهُ لَمْ يَجْلِسْ بَعْدَ السَّجْدَةِ الثَّانِيَةِ، وَيَدُلُّ عَلَيْهِ اَنَّ طَائِفَةً مِّنَ الْحُفَّاظِ ذَكَرُوْا أَنَّ حَدِيْثَ أَبِي حُمَيْدٍ لَيْسَ فِيْهِ ذِكْرُ هَذِهِ الْجَلْسَةِ.

217 Ibn Rajab's *Fatḥ al-Bārī*, 5:142; *Natā'ij al-Afkār*, 2:132.

218 *Al-Tamhīd*, 7:160.

219 *Abū Dāwūd* (733).

This narration clearly states that he ﷺ did not sit after the second *sajdah*. The evidence for this is that a group of ḥadīth experts (*ḥuffāẓ*) said there is no mention of this sitting in the ḥadīth of Abū Ḥumayd.[220]

Imām Ibn al-Mundhir (d. 318 AH) and Imām Ibn ʿAbd al-Barr (d. 463 AH) report from Imām Aḥmad (d. 241 AH):

أَكْثَرُ الْأَحَادِيْثِ عَلَى هٰذَا.

Most of the ḥadīths prove this (i.e., one should stand up after the second *sajdah* without sitting).[221]

Hence, not performing the *jalsah istirāḥah* after the second *sajdah* is the *sunnah* practice of Rasūlullāh ﷺ, and it was also the practice of most of the Ṣaḥābah.[222] As for the narration that mentions the *jalsah istirāḥah*, according to the majority of scholars it is due to a certain excuse, in contrast to the general habit of Rasūlullāh ﷺ.[223] Shaykh Muḥammad ibn ʿAbd al-Wahhāb also interpreted this narration to be based upon a certain excuse (*ʿudhr*).[224]

Ḥadīth 24
THE *SUNNAH* METHOD OF SITTING (*QAʿDAH*) FOR MEN

It is necessary to sit after every two *rakʿahs* for *tashahhud*. The sunnah method of sitting (*qaʿdah*) for *tashahhud*, with respect

---

220 *Fatḥ al-Bārī*, 5:139; *al-Tamhīd*, 7:161.
221 *Al-Awsaṭ*, 3:365; *al-Tamhīd*, 7:160.
222 *Muṣannaf Ibn Abī Shaybah*, 1:431.
223 *Al-Jawḥar al-Naqiyy*, 2:211.
224 *Muʾallafāt al-Shaykh Muḥammad ibn ʿAbd al-Wahhāb*, 4:95.

to men, is explained in the following ḥadīth of Sayyida ʿĀ'ishah ﵂, wherein she narrates:

وَكَانَ يَقُوْلُ فِىْ كُلِّ رَكْعَتَيْنِ التَّحِيَّةَ، وَكَانَ يَفْرِشُ رِجْلَهُ الْيُسْرَى، وَيَنْصِبُ رِجْلَهُ الْيُمْنَى.

Rasūlullāh ﷺ would recite the *taḥiyyah* (complete *tashahhud*) after every two *rakʿahs*, and he would spread his left foot and keep his right foot upright.[225]

The aforementioned narration of Sayyidah ʿĀ'ishah ﵂ includes Rasūlullāh's ﷺ sittings (*qaʿdahs*), both the first and the second, as she has explained only one method of sitting (*qaʿdah*) which is not exclusive to the first sitting (*qaʿdah*) alone. As for those who say this ḥadīth is exclusive to the first sitting (*qaʿdah*), ʿAllāmah al-Shawkānī (d. 1255 AH) has written in response to them:

أَنَّ رُوَاتَهَا ذَكَرُوْا هَذِهِ الصِّفَّةَ لِجُلُوْسِ التَّشَهُّدِ وَلَمْ يُقَيِّدُوْهُ بِالْأَوَّلِ، وَاقْتِصَارُهُمْ عَلَيْهَا مِنْ - دُوْنِ تَعَرُّضٍ لِّذِكْرِ غَيْرِهَا - مُشْعِرٌ بِأَنَّهَا هِيَ الْهَيْئَةُ الْمَشْرُوْعَةُ فِي التَّشَهُّدَيْنِ جَمِيْعًا، وَلَوْ كَانَتْ مُخْتَصَّةً بِالْأَوَّلِ لَذَكَرُوْا هَيْئَةَ التَّشَهُّدِ الْأَخِيْرِ وَلَمْ يُهْمِلُوْهُ، لَاسِيَّمَا وَهُمْ بِصَدَدِ بَيَانِ صَلَوةِ رَسُوْلِ اللهِ وَتَعْلِيْمِهِ لِمَنْ لَايُحْسِنُ الصَّلَاةَ، فَعُلِمَ بِذَلِكَ أَنَّ الْهَيْئَةَ شَامِلَةٌ لَهُمَا.

The narrators of this ḥadīth mentioned this description of sitting for *tashahhud* without confining it to the first sitting. Their sufficing upon this description without mentioning anything else indicates it is the only legislated method in both sittings. If this description was exclusive to the first sitting, they would have mentioned the manner of the second sitting and not left it out, especially when they

225 *Muslim* (1109).

> are actually explaining the ṣalāh of Rasūlullāh's ﷺ, and how he taught it to the person who could not perform it properly. Therefore, it is understood that this method covers both sittings.[226]

Mawlānā Nawāb Nūr al-Ḥasan (d. 1336 AH) has derived the same ruling from this ḥadīth.[227]

❧

Ḥadīth 25
THE *SUNNAH* METHOD OF SITTING (*QAʿDAH*) FOR WOMEN

The method of sitting in *qaʿdah* for women is different to that of men. Al-Imām al-Aʿẓam Abū Ḥanīfah ﵀ narrates from Imām Nāfiʿ ﵀ that Sayyidunā ʿAbdullāh ibn ʿUmar ﵄ was asked:

كَيْفَ كُنَّ النِّسَاءُ يُصَلِّيْنَ عَلَى عَهْدِ رَسُوْلِ اللهِ؟ قَالَ: كُنَّ يَتَرَبَّعْنَ، ثُمَّ أُمِرْنَ أَنْ يَحْتَفِزْنَ.

> How did women perform ṣalāh (when sitting in *qaʿdāh*) in the time of Rasūlullāh ﷺ? He replied, "They would sit cross-legged, then they were instructed to sit on their buttocks (and take their feet out towards the right)."[228]

The chain of transmission of this ḥadīth is rigorously authentic, as both al-Imām al-Aʿẓam Abū Ḥanīfah ﵀ and Imām Nāfiʿ ﵀ are reputable Tābiʿūn and reliable ḥadīth scholars

---

226 *Nayl al-Awṭār*, 1:422.

227 *Fatḥ al-ʿAllām*, p.173.

228 Ḥaṣkafī's *Musnad al-Imām al-Aʿẓam*, p. 73; Ḥārithī's *Musnad Abī Ḥanīfah* (79); Imām al-Khawārzamī's *Jāmiʿ al-Masānīd*, 1:400.

(*muḥaddithūn*), and Sayyidunā ʿAbdullāh ibn ʿUmar ﵄ is a famous Ṣaḥābī. This ḥadīth can be found in *Musnad al-Imām al-Aʿẓam*, as compiled by al-Ḥārithī and others. Imām al-Ḥārithī has been classified as reliable by Ḥāfiẓ Ibn Ḥajar and other ḥadīth scholars (*muḥaddithūn*), and his *musnad* is reliable and authentic.[229]

Mawlānā Nadhīr Ḥusayn, and his students, have also deemed the *Musnad al-Imām al-Aʿẓam* to be from the reliable ḥadīth compilations.[230]

In addition to the above, this ḥadīth has been reported from Sayyidunā ʿAbdullāh ibn ʿUmar ﵄, through another chain, in which Rasūlullāh ﷺ said:

إِذَا جَلَسَتِ الْمَرْأَةُ فِي الصَّلَاةِ وَضَعَتْ فَخِذَهَا عَلَى فَخِذِهَا الْأُخْرَى، وَإِذَا سَجَدَتْ أَلْصَقَتْ بَطْنَهَا بِفَخِذَيْهَا، كَأَسْتَرِ مَا يَكُوْنُ لَهَا، وَإِنَّ اللهَ تَعَالَى يَنْظُرُ إِلَيْهَا، وَيَقُوْلُ: يَا مَلَائِكَتِي، أُشْهِدُكُمْ أَنِّيْ قَدْ غَفَرْتُ لَهَا.

When a woman sits in ṣalāh, she should place one thigh on the other. When she performs *sajdah*, she should join her stomach with her thighs, as concealing as is possible for her. Allāh looks at her and says: "O my angels! I make you witness that I have forgiven her."[231]

Sayyidunā ʿAbdullāh ibn ʿAbbās's ﵄ verdict also further strengthens these narrations.[232] Also, Mawlānā ʿAbd al-Jabbār Ghaznawī deemed it better for women to extend their feet towards the right when sitting, as it is more concealing.[233]

---

229 For further details, refer to the author's book: *Imām Aʿẓam Abū Ḥanīfah ka Muḥaddithānah Maqām* (p. 535-541).

230 *Fatāwā Nadhīriyyah*, 1:243.

231 Abū Nuʿaym's *Tarīkh Aṣbahān*, 1:200.

232 *Muṣannaf Ibn Abī Shaybah*, 2:302.

233 *Fatāwā ʿUlamā'-i-Ḥadīth*, 3:149.

Ḥadīth 26
THE *SUNNAH* METHOD OF *QAʿDAH* AND THE *SUNNAH* WORDING OF *TASHAHHUD*

The following ḥadīth, reported by Sayyidunā ʿAbdullāh ibn Zubayr رضي الله عنه, states that one should place their hands on their thighs in *tashahhud*:

كَانَ رَسُوْلُ اللهِ ﷺ إِذَا قَعَدَ يَدْعُوْ وَضَعَ يَدَهُ الْيُمْنَى عَلَى فَخِذِهِ الْيُمْنَى، وَيَدَهُ الْيُسْرَى عَلَى فَخِذِهِ الْيُسْرَى، وَأَشَارَ بِأُصْبُعِهِ السَّبَّابَةِ، وَوَضَعَ إِبْهَامَهُ عَلَى أُصْبُعِهِ الْوُسْطَى، وَيُلْقِمُ كَفَّهُ الْيُسْرَى رُكْبَتَهُ.

When Rasūlullāh ﷺ sat to supplicate, he placed his right hand on his right thigh and his left hand on his left thigh. He pointed with his forefinger, placing his thumb on his middle finger, and held his knee with the palm of his left hand.[234]

This ḥadīth mentions that Rasūlullāh ﷺ supplicated in the sitting (*qaʿdah*). The most authentic words of *tashahhud* reported from Rasūlullāh ﷺ are as follows:

اَلتَّحِيَّاتُ لِلّٰهِ وَالصَّلَوَاتُ وَالطَّيِّبَاتُ، اَلسَّلَامُ عَلَيْكَ أَيُّهَا النَّبِيُّ وَرَحْمَةُ اللهِ وَبَرَكَاتُهُ، اَلسَّلَامُ عَلَيْنَا وَعَلَى عِبَادِ اللهِ الصَّالِحِيْنَ، أَشْهَدُ أَنْ لَّا إِلٰهَ إِلَّا اللهُ وَأَشْهَدُ أَنَّ مُحَمَّدًا عَبْدُهُ وَرَسُوْلُهُ.

All greetings, salutations and pure things are for Allāh. Peace be on you, O Prophet, and Allāh's mercy and blessings. Peace be on us and the righteous slaves of Allāh. I testify there is no god besides Allāh, and I testify that Muḥammad ﷺ is His slave and messenger.[235]

234 Muslim (1307)

235 *Bukhārī* (831), *Muslim* (827).

The *sunnah* method of reciting these words is that in a ṣalāh that consists of two *qaʿdahs* (i.e., three or four *rakʿahs*), one will recite these words only in the first *qaʿdah*. In the second *qaʿdah*, and also in a ṣalāh that only has one qaʿdah (i.e., two *rakʿahs*), one will send blesssings on Rasūlullāh ﷺ and add one or more supplications after the words of *tashahhud*. Mawlānā ʿAbdullāh Rawparī's (d. 1384 AH) research proves the same,[236] and this was the opinion of ʿAllāmah al-Shawkānī (d. 1255 AH).[237]

❧

Ḥadīth 27

THE *SUNNAH* METHOD OF INDICATING WITH THE FOREFINGER IN *TASHAHHUD*

When one is reciting the *tashahhud* and reaches the words of testimony (*shahādah*), one should indicate with the forefinger of the right hand, as reported in the following ḥadīth of Sayyidunā ʿAbdullāh ibn Zubayr رضي الله عنهما:

أَنَّ النَّبِيَّ ﷺ كَانَ يُشِيْرُ بِأُصْبُعِهِ إِذَا دَعَا، وَلَا يُحَرِّكُهَا.

> When Nabī ﷺ would supplicate (i.e., the words of *shahādah*), he would indicate with his forefinger and not move it.[238]

Imām al-Nawawī (d. 676 AH) said: "Abū Dawūd has narrated it with an authentic chain."[239] Imām Ibn ʿAbd al-Barr (d. 463 AH) deemed this ḥadīth to be authentic (*ṣaḥih*), and Imām al-Baghawī (d. 516 AH) classified it as sound (*ḥasan*).[240]

---

236 *Fatāwā Ahl-i-Ḥadīth*, 1:528; *Fatāwā ʿUlamā'-i-Ḥadīth*, 3:176.

237 *Nayl al-Awṭār*, 1:430-431.

238 *Abū Dāwūd* (989); *Ṣaḥih Abī ʿAwānah* (1594).

239 *Sharḥ al-Muhadhdhab*, 3:454.

240 *Al-Istidhkār*, 1:478; *Maṣābīḥ al-Sunnah*, 1:115.

Furthermore, this ḥadīth was narrated by Imām Abū ʿAwānah (d. 316 AH) in his *Ṣaḥīh*, which is evidence of its authenticity, as acknowledged by non-muqallid scholars. Mawlānā ʿAbd al-Raḥmān Mubārakpūrī, Mawlānā ʿAbdullāh Rawparī, Mawlānā Abū Yaḥyā Shāhjahānpūrī*, Mawlānā ʿAbd al-Salām Mubārakpūrī*, Mawlānā Muḥammad Jānbāz Ḥayderābādī*, and others amongst their senior scholars, clearly said Imām Abū ʿAwānah has adhered to authentic narrations in his *Ṣaḥīh*, and all the narrations in his compilation are authentic (*ṣaḥīh*).[241]

Despite these clear statements of authenticity from the senior non-muqallid scholars, some of the juniors amongst them accuse Muḥammad ibn ʿAjlān, the narrator of this ḥadīth, of *tadlīs* (although he is reliable according to the majority of ḥadīth scholars (*muḥaddithūn*), as acknowledged by the non-muqallids).[242] Mawlānā Muḥibullāh Rāshidī stated that when ḥadīth scholars (*muḥaddithūn*) authenticate the ḥadīth of a *mudallis*, it is established according to them that the narrator did not do *tadlīs* in that ḥadīth.[243]

Furthermore, this narration of Muḥammad ibn ʿAjlān is supported by the narration of ʿAmr ibn Dīnār. Also, Sayyidunā ʿAbdullāh ibn ʿUmar ؓ has reported this ḥadīth from Rasūlullāh ﷺ with the same words, which has been authenticated by Imām al-Dāraquṭnī (d. 385 AH).[244]

Similarly, it is supported by those authentic narrations that state that Rasūlullāh ﷺ indicated with his forefinger, rather than moving it, as mentioned under ḥadīth twenty-six. Hence, any objection made on this ḥadīth because of Muḥammad ibn ʿAjlān will be totally invalid.

---

241 *Taḥqīq al-Kalām*, 2:122; *Risālah Rafʿ Yadayn Aur Āmīn*, p. 22; *al-Irshād ilā Sabīl al-Rashād*, p. 249; *Sīrat al-Bukhārī*, p. 14; *Fatāwā ʿUlamā'-i-Ḥadīth*, 94.

242 *ʿAwn al-Maʿbūd*, 1:389.

243 *Maqālāt Rāshidiyyah*, 1:338.

244 *Kitāb al-ʿIlal* (2899).

This authentic narration clearly negates one constantly moving their forefinger when reciting the words of *shahādah*, whereas the narration reported by Sayyidunā Wā'il ibn Ḥujr ﷺ, with the words "he would move it (*yuḥarrikuhā*)" suggest that Rasūlullāh ﷺ constantly moved his forefinger.

Reconciling these narrations is possible, by interpreting the word *yuḥarrikuhā* as a single movement of indication, not constant movement. This is because the action of indicating consists of slight movement, which has been described by the narrator as moving. This is how the narrations have been reconciled by Imām al-Nasā'ī (d. 303 AH) and Imām al-Bayhaqī (d. 458 AH).[245]

ʿAllāmah al-Shawkānī (d. 1255 AH), ʿAllāmah Amīr al-Ṣanʿānī (d. 1182 AH), Mawlānā Muḥammad Punjābī* (d. 1315 AH), Mawlānā ʿAṭā'ullāh Ḥanīf (d. 1409 AH), Mawlānā Nūr al-Ḥasan ibn Nawāb Ṣiddīq Ḥasan Khān (d. 1336 AH), and others also preferred this reconciliation.[246]

In addition, ʿAllāmah Ibn Ḥazm al-Ẓāhirī (d. 456 AH) and ʿAllāmah Waḥīd al-Zamān (d. 1338 AH) stated that it is preferable for one who is reciting the words of *tashahhud* to indicate with his forefinger and not constantly move it.[247]

The method of indicating is that on reaching the words: أَشْهَدُ أَنْ لَّا اِلٰهَ اِلَّا اللهُ, make a circle with the right hand using the thumb and middle finger, as mentioned under ḥadīth twenty-six. When saying the words: أَشْهَدُ أَنْ لَّا اِلٰهَ, the forefinger should be raised, and on reaching the words: اِلَّا اللهُ the forefinger should be lowered, so that his action, statement and beliefs all testify to Allāh's oneness.[248]

---

245 *Nasā'ī* with *al-Taʿlīqāt al-Salafiyyah* (1276); *al-Sunan al-Kubrā*, 2:132.

246 *Nayl al-Awṭār*, 1:428; *Subul al-Salām*, 1:198; *al-Taʿlīqāt al-Salafiyyah*, 2:236; *Fatḥ al-ʿAllām*, p. 197.

247 *Al-Muḥallā*, 4:97; *Nuzul al-Abrār*, 1:81.

248 *Subul al-Salām*, 1:198; *Nayl al-Awṭār*, 1:429; *Fatḥ al-ʿAllām*, p. 197.

Mawlānā Muḥammad Ṣādiq Siyālkawtī writes: "In accordance to the beloved *sunnah* of our beloved Rasūl ﷺ, one should lift the forefinger, such that when one reaches the *shahādah*, a circle should be made by placing the thumb on his middle finger. The forefinger should be lifted as soon as the word: أَشْهَدُ is read (thus affirming Allāh's oneness with one's finger as well as the tongue) and then it should be put down on the word: اِلَّا اللهُ. It is as though the slave is in the court of the Lord of all lords in the sitting position, and he is giving testimony to Allāh's oneness, sincerely with his heart, so that this sincere testimony becomes the means of the Knower of the Unseen (*ʿAllām al-ghuyūb*) being pleased, and so that with the intention of testifying to Allāh's oneness, the unsheathed sword, i.e., the finger, wounds the satan and makes him despondent."[249]

❧

Ḥadīth 28

THE *SUNNAH* METHOD OF SAYING *SALĀM*

When a person completes his supplication in *qaʿdah*, he should turn his face to the right and say the words:

اَلسَّلَامُ عَلَيْكُمْ وَرَحْمَةُ اللهِ.

Then he should turn his face to the left and say the same words.

Sayyidunā ʿAbdullāh ibn Masʿūd رضي الله عنه narrates:

أَنَّهُ كَانَ يُسَلِّمُ عَنْ يَمِيْنِهِ وَعَنْ يَسَارِهِ: اَلسَّلَامُ عَلَيْكُمْ وَرَحْمَةُ اللهِ، اَلسَّلَامُ عَلَيْكُمْ وَرَحْمَةُ اللهِ.

249 *Ṣalāt al-Rasūl*, p. 268-269.

He ﷺ would say *salām* to the right and left (saying): Peace be upon you and Allāh's mercy, Peace be upon you and Allāh's mercy.[250]

Imām al-Tirmidhī (d. 279 AH) narrated this ḥadīth in his *Sunan* and then said: "The ḥadīth of Ibn Masʿūd is a sound, authentic ḥadīth."

Ḥadīth 29
THE METHOD OF PROSTRATION FOR A LAPSE (*SAJDAT AL-SAHW*)

If one forgets to perform an obligatory (*wājib*) action in ṣalāh; delays or brings forward a compulsory (*farḍ*) or obligatory (*wājib*) action; or has doubt in the number of *rakʿahs* he has performed, performing the prostration of lapse (*sajdat al-sahw)* in these scenarios will ensure the ṣalāh is valid.

The method of *sajdat al-sahw* is as follows: In the final sitting (*qaʿdāh*) after reciting *tashahhud*, the person will make salām once to the right and then perform two prostrations. Thereafter, he will recite *tashahhud*, send blessings upon Rasūlullāh ﷺ, supplicate, and complete his ṣalāh by saying *salām* to both sides. This method is established from many authentic narrations, one of them being the ḥadīth of Sayyidunā ʿAbdullāh ibn Masʿūd رضي الله عنه wherein he narrates from Rasūlullāh ﷺ:

إِذَا صَلَّى أَحَدُكُمْ فَلَمْ يَدْرِ أَثَلَاثًا أَمْ أَرْبَعًا، فَلْيَنْظُرْ أَحْرَى ذَلِكَ إِلَى الصَّوَابِ فَلْيُتِمَّهُ، ثُمَّ لِيُسَلِّمْ، ثُمَّ لِيَسْجُدْ سَجْدَتَيِ السَّهْوِ وَيَتَشَهَّدْ وَيُسَلِّمْ.

250 *Tirmidhī* (295).

> If one of you performs ṣalāh but does not know if he has performed three or four *rakʿahs*, he should consider which of them is more likely to be correct, and then complete his ṣalāh accordingly. He should perform *salām*, then perform the two *sajdahs* of lapse (*sajdat al-sahw*), recite *tashahhud* (and send salutation upon Rasūlullāh ﷺ and supplicate) and perform *salām*.[251]

This ḥadīth is rigorously authentic. All its narrators are reliable and great imāms, and narrators of *Ṣaḥīḥ al-Bukhārī* and *Ṣaḥīḥ Muslim*, except Rabīʿ ibn Sulaymān al-Mu'adhdhin, a student of Imām al-Shāfiʿī, who is also authentic.[252]

Apart from this ḥadīth, the evidence of reciting *tashahhud* after *sajdat al-sahw* is also established from the ḥadīth of Sayyidunā ʿImrān ibn Ḥuṣayn ﷺ,[253] as well as many other narrations. Imām al-Tirmidhī has classified this ḥadīth as sound (*ḥasan*), and according to some manuscripts of *Sunan al-Tirmidhī*, it is sound (*ḥasan*) and authentic (*ṣaḥīḥ*).[254] Imām al-Ḥākim (d. 405 AH) and Imām al-Dhahabī (d. 748 AH) deemed it to conform to the criteria of Imām al-Bukhārī and Imām Muslim ﷺ.[255]

Shaykh Nāṣir al-Dīn Albānī said:

لٰكِنْ مَجْمُوْعَهَا قَدْ يُعْطِي قُوَّةً.

The total sum of the narrations give strength.[256]

In addition, Shaykh al-Albānī classified them as sound (*ḥasan*).[257] Mawlānā Shams al-Ḥaqq ʿAẓimābādī also graded

251 *Sharḥ Maʿānī al-Āthār*, 1:294.

252 *Taqrīb al-Tahdhīb*, 1:294.

253 *Tirmidhī* (395).

254 *Mishkāt al-Maṣābīḥ*, ed. Nāṣir al-Dīn al-Albānī, 1:322.

255 *Mustadrak al-Ḥākim*, 1:470.

256 *Mishkāt al-Maṣābīḥ*, ed. Nāṣir al-Dīn al-Albānī, 1:322.

257 *Irwā' al-Ghalīl*, 2:129.

them as sound (*ḥasan*).[258] Also, apart from the above ḥadīth, saying the salām twice, before and after the *sajdat al-sahw*, is established from several authentic narrations.[259]

It should be noted that the narrations are clear that the *salām* at the end of ṣalāh should be said twice, as mentioned under ḥadīth twenty-eight. However, the narrations do not clearly mention how many times the *salām* should be said before the *sajdat al-sahw*: whether it is to the right and left, or will only one to the right suffice.

Some jurists (*fuqahā'*) suggest that even before the *sajdat al-sahw, salām* should be said twice. However, the majority of the jurists (*fuqahā'*) are of the opinion that saying it only once to the right is preferable, as the *salām* at this point is for exiting the ṣalāh (*taḥlīl*) which is legislated only once to the right. On the other hand, the *salām* to the left is to give greetings (*taḥiyyah*) to the people that are praying and the angels, which is not needed at this point, as the appropriate place for this is at the end of the ṣalāh.[260]

❧

Ḥadīth 30
IT IS *SUNNAH* TO RAISE THE HANDS AND SUPPLICATE AFTER THE OBLIGATORY ṢALĀH

The time after the obligatory ṣalāh is when supplication (*duʿā'*) is accepted. Whatever supplication is made at this time is answered by Allāh ﷻ. At this point, it is *sunnah* for the imām and follower (*muqtadī*) to raise their hands and make *duʿā* in

---

258 *ʿAwn al-Maʿbūd*, 2:373.
259 *Ṣaḥīh Muslim* (1231, 1232).
260 *Radd al-Muḥtār*, 1:545-546.

congregation, as proven from the following ḥadīth, in which Muḥammad ibn Abū Yaḥyā ﵀ said:

رَأَيْتُ عَبْدَ اللهِ بْنَ الزُّبَيْرَ ﵄، وَرَأَى رَجُلًا رَافِعًا يَدَيْهِ يَدْعُوْ قَبْلَ أَنْ يَّفْرُغَ مِنْ صَلَاتِهِ، فَلَمَّا فَرَغَ مِنْهَا قَالَ: إِنَّ رَسُوْلَ اللهِ ﷺ لَمْ يَكُنْ يَرْفَعُ يَدَيْهِ حَتَّى يَفْرُغَ مِنْ صَلَاتِهِ.

> I saw ʿAbdullāh ibn Zubayr ﵄ observing a man who was raising his hands and supplicating before he had completed his ṣalāh. When he completed his ṣalāh, ʿAbdullāh ibn Zubayr ﵄ said to him: "Rasūlullāh ﷺ would not raise his hands until he had completed his ṣalāh."[261]

Ḥāfiẓ Nūr al-Dīn al-Haythamī (d. 807 AH) and Ḥāfiẓ Jalāl al-Dīn al-Suyūṭī (d. 911 AH) say the narrators of this ḥadīth are reliable.[262] Ḥāfiẓ Ibn Ḥajar al-ʿAsqalānī (d. 852 AH) classified this ḥadīth as sound (*ḥasan*).[263] Imām Ḍiyā al-Dīn al-Maqdisī (d. 643 AH) cited this ḥadīth in *al-Mukhtārah*,[264] which proves its authenticity according to Imām al-Maqdisī, as stated by Mawlānā Irshād al-Ḥaqq al-Atharī.[265]

Mawlānā Irshād al-Ḥaqq al-Atharī also deemed the ḥadīth sound and capable of using for evidence, and has defended its narrators (Sulaymān ibn al-Ḥasan al-ʿAṭṭār, Fuḍayl ibn Sulaymān, and others) in great detail.[266]

It is clear from the aforementioned authentic ḥadīth that raising the hands for supplication after the obligatory ṣalāh is

261 *Al-Muʿjam al-Kabīr* (14912).

262 *Majmaʿ al-Zawāʾid*, 10:310; *Faḍḍ al-Wiʿāʾ*, p. 86.

263 *Natāʾij al-Afkār*, 2:310, quoted from Shaykh ʿAbd al-Hafīẓ Makkī's *Istiḥbāb al-Duʿāʾ Baʿd al-Farāʾiḍ wa Raf al-Yadayn Fīhi*, p. 103.

264 *Al-Aḥādīth al-Mukhtārah*, 9:336.

265 *Maqālāt*, 2:263.

266 Ibid, 2:260-273.

the *sunnah* of Rasūlullāh ﷺ, and it is also evidence for congregational supplication, as it cannot be imagined that Rasūlullāh ﷺ raised his hands after leading the congregational ṣalāh, whilst the noble Ṣaḥābah ﷺ, who were aware of the virtue of supplication after obligatory ṣalāh and had heard its reward from Rasūlullāh ﷺ, did not join him. If anyone claims otherwise, then the burden of proof is upon them.

There are other ḥadīths that prove congregational supplication after the obligatory ṣalāh. Mawlānā Muḥibbullāh Shāh Rāshidī has written a separate article, in which he has proven that congregational supplication after the obligatory ṣalāh is *sunnah* both for the imām and followers. He has used the aforesaid ḥadīth, and other narrations, as evidence.[267]

Moreover, Mawlānā Nadhīr Ḥusain al-Dihlawī, Mawlānā ʿAbd al-Raḥmān Mubārakpūrī, Mawlānā ʿAbdullāh Rawparī, Mawlānā ʿAbd al-Jabbār Ghaznawī, Mawlānā Muḥammad Ṣādiq Siyālkowtī and others considered congregational supplication by raising the hands after obligatory ṣalāh as permissible.[268]

It should be noted that just as raising the hands for supplication is *sunnah*, wiping one's hands over the face after completing the supplication is also *sunnah*. Sayyidunā ʿUmar ﷺ reports that when Rasūlullāh ﷺ used to raise his hands for supplication, he would not put them down until he had wiped them over his face.

Imām al-Tirmidhī and Imām al-Baghawī deemed this ḥadīth to be authentic, and Ḥāfiẓ Ibn Ḥajar classified it as sound (*ḥasan*).[269] Similar narrations have also been transmitted from Sayyidunā Ibn ʿAbbās ﷺ and Sayyidunā Walīd ibn ʿAbdullāh

267 *Maqālāt Rāshidiyyah*, 1:106-114.

268 *Fatāwā Nadhīriyyah*, 1:566; *Tuḥfat al-Aḥwadhī*, 1:246; *Fatāwā Ahl-i-Ḥadīth*, 1:530-531; *Fatāwā ʿUlamā-i-Ḥadīth*, 3:214-222; *Ṣalāt al-Raṣūl* ﷺ, p. 311.

269 *Tirmidhī* (3386); *Maṣābīḥ al-Sunnah* (1549); *Bulūgh al-Marām* (1475).

ﷺ.[270] Ḥāfiẓ Ibn Ḥajar considered the narration of Sayyidunā Ibn ʿAbbās ﷺ to be sound (*ḥasan*).[271]

The reputable Tābiʿī, Imām al-Zuhrī ﷺ, narrated this ḥadīth as a *mursal* narration,[272] which will be classified as a supported (*muʿtaḍad*) *mursal* narration, due to the aforesaid supporting narrations. This type of *mursal* is evidence according to all scholars, as mentioned under ḥadīth twenty-two.

In addition to this, Imām al-Bukhārī ﷺ has reported with an authentic chain, from Sayyidunā ʿAbdullāh ibn ʿUmar ﷺ and Sayyidunā ʿAbdullāh ibn Zubayr ﷺ, that they would wipe their hands over their faces after supplication.[273] ʿAllāmah Amīr al-Ṣanʿānī, ʿAllāmah Nūr al-Ḥasan, Mawlānā Irshād al-Ḥaqq al-Atharī, amongst others considered it a legislated (*mashrūʿ*) and *sunnah* action.[274]

❧

Ḥadīth 31

WITR ṢALĀH IS THREE *RAKʿAHS* WITH ONE *SALĀM*

After the ʿishā obligatory (*farḍ*) ṣalāh and the two *sunnah*, performing the three *rakʿahs* of witr is compulsory (*wājib*). The three *rakʿahs* will be performed with *salām* at the end (i.e, three *rakʿahs* together). Its method is that after the second rakʿah one will sit for *tashahhud*, and after completing *tashahhud*, one will stand for the third *rakʿah*. This *rakʿah* will then be completed with *salām* at the end of the qaʿdah.

270 *Mustadrak al-Ḥākim*, 1:720, Ṭabarānī's *Kitāb al-Duʿā'* (214).

271 *Faḍḍ al-Wiʿā'*, p. 76.

272 *Muṣannaf ʿAbd al-Razzāq*, 2:161.

273 *Al-Adab al-Mufrad* (609).

274 *Subul al-Salām*, 4:321; *Fatḥ al-ʿAllām*, p. 996; *Maqālāt*, 1:261-270.

Sayyidah ʿĀ'ishah ﵂ narrates:

كَانَ رَسُوْلُ اللهِ ﷺ يُوْتِرُ بِثَلَاثٍ، لَا يُسَلِّمُ إِلَّا فِيْ آخِرِهِنَّ. قَالَ الْحَاكِمُ: وَهَذَا وِتْرُ أَمِيْرِ الْمُؤْمِنِيْنَ عُمَرَ بْنِ الْخَطَّابِ ﵁ وَعَنْهُ أَخَذَهُ أَهْلُ الْمَدِيْنَةِ.

Rasūlullāh ﷺ would perform three *rakʿahs* of witr, and he would only make salām at the end.

Imām al-Ḥākim said, "This is the witr of the Leader of the believers (*Amīr al-Mu'minīn*) ʿUmar ﵁, and the people of Madīnah took this from him."[275] Imām al-Dhahabī remained silent upon this ḥadīth in *Talkhīṣ al-Mustadrak.*[276]

Mawlānā ʿAbdullāh Rawparī and Mawlānā ʿAṭā'ullāh Ḥanīf said that a ḥadīth upon which al-Dhahabī remains silent in his *Mukhtaṣar* (*Talkhīṣ al-Mustadrak*) is authentic according to him.[277]

The objection of *tadlīs* on the narrator of this ḥadīth, Abū Qatādah, will be answered under ḥadīth thirty-five. Also, this ḥadīth has been narrated by Sayyidunā Ubayy ibn Kaʿb ﵁,[278] and has been authenticated by Ḥāfiẓ Ibn Ḥajar.[279] Also, ḥadith thirty-two supports this.

Similarly, it is supported by the ḥadith of Sayyidah ʿĀ'ishah ﵂ in which she states:

كَانَ رَسُوْلُ اللهِ ﷺ لَا يُسَلِّمُ فِي الرَّكْعَتَيْنِ الْأُوْلَيَيْنِ مِنَ الْوِتْرِ.

Rasūlullāh ﷺ would not make salām after the first two *rakʿahs* of witr.[280]

275 *Mustadrak al-Ḥākim* (1140).

276 Ibid.

277 *Fatāwā Ahl-i-Ḥadīth*, 1:635. *Fatāwā ʿUlamā-i-Ḥadīth*, 3:190.

278 *Nasā'ī* (1703).

279 *Fatḥ al-Bārī*, 2:611.

280 *Mustadrak al-Ḥākim*, 1:446.

Imām al-Ḥākim (d. 405 AH) and Imām al-Dhahabī (d. 748 AH) both deemed this ḥadith to be in accordance to the criteria of Imām al-Bukhārī ﵀ and Imām Muslim ﵀.[281]

Sitting in the second *rakʿah* for *tashahhud* in witr ṣalāh is established from ḥadīth twenty-four, in which Sayyidah ʿĀ'ishah ﵂ states:

كَانَ يَقُوْلُ فِيْ كُلِّ رَكْعَتَيْنِ التَّحِيَّةَ.

Rasūlullāh ﷺ would recite *al-taḥiyyah* (complete *tashahhud*) after every two *rakʿahs.*

This ḥadīth clearly explains the general ruling of all the ṣalāhs of Rasūlullāh ﷺ, i.e., that he would perform tashah-hud after every two *rakʿahs*, and it does not exclude the witr ṣalāh. Based on this ḥadīth, performing qaʿdah and reciting tashahhud in the second *rakʿah* of witr will be necessary. It is also clear from this that Rasūlullāh ﷺ performing only one *rakʿah* of witr is not clearly established from any verbal (*qawlī*) narration or ḥadith that reports his action (*fiʿlī*).

The famous Shāfiʿī ḥadīth scholar (*muḥaddith*), Ḥāfiẓ Ibn al-Ṣalāh (d. 643 AH) stated:

لَا نَعلَمُ فِيْ رِوَايَاتِ الْوِتْرِ، مَعَ كَثْرَتِهَا، أَنَّهُ عَلَيْهِ السَّلَامُ أَوْتَرَ بِرَكْعَةٍ فَحَسْبُ.

Despite there being many narrations regarding witr, we do not know of any narration that states that he ﷺ only performed one *rakʿah* of witr.[282]

Some who consider witr to be one *rakʿah* substantiate using the narration containing the words:

صَلِّ رَكْعَةً وَّاحِدَةً.

Perform one *rakʿah.*

281 Ibid.

282 *Talkhīṣ al-Ḥabīr*, 2:15.

However, Ḥāfiẓ Ibn Ḥajar al-ʿAsqalānī (d. 852 AH) has refuted this proof with the following words:

وَتُعُقِّبَ بِأَنَّهُ لَيْسَ صَرِيْحًا فِي الفَصْلِ، فَيَحْتَمِلُ أَنْ يُرِيْدَ بِقَوْلِهِ صَلِّ رَكْعَةً وَاحِدَةً، أَيْ مُضَافَةً إِلَى رَكْعَتَيْنِ مِمَّا مَضَى.

This has been countered, because the narration is not clear regarding reading (one *rakʿah*) separately. It is possible that the statement: "perform one *rakʿah*" means by adding to the two previous *rakʿahs.*[283]

Similarly, all the narrations which suggest Rasūlullāh ﷺ performed one *rakʿāh* of witr will mean that he ﷺ added a rakʿāh to the two *rakʿāhs*, not that he sufficed on just one *rakʿāh.* This is how the narrations are reconciled. Thus, one should not suffice on performing only one *rakʿāh* of witr.

Ḥadīth 32

IT IS *SUNNAH* TO READ THE SUPPLICATION OF *QUNŪT* BEFORE *RUKŪʿ*

In the third *rakʿah* of witr, after reciting *Sūrat al-Fātiḥah* and a *sūrah*, one will say the *takbīr* by raising the hands (then fold them) and read the supplication (*duʿā'*) of *qunūt* whilst standing. After completing *qunūt*, one should go into *rukūʿ*. This method is established from Rasūlullāh ﷺ in the following ḥadīth:

أَنَّ رَسُوْلَ اللهِ ﷺ كَانَ يُوْتِرُ بِثَلَاثِ رَكَعَاتٍ، كَانَ يَقْرَأُ فِي الْأُوْلَى بِـ(سَبِّحِ اسْمَ رَبِّكَ الْأَعْلَى)، وَفِي الثَّانِيَةِ بِـ(قُلْ يَا أَيُّهَا الْكٰفِرُوْنَ)، وَفِي الثَّالِثَةِ: بِـ(قُلْ هُوَ اللهُ أَحَدٌ)، وَيَقْنُتُ قَبْلَ الرُّكُوْعِ.

283 *Fatḥ al-Bārī*, 2:610.

Rasūlullāh ﷺ would perform three *rakʿahs* of *witr*. He would recite *Sūrat al-Aʿlā* in the first *rakʿah*, *Sūrat al-Kāfirūn* in the second *rakʿah* and *Sūrat al-Ikhlāṣ* in the third *rakʿah*. He would recite *qunūt* before the *rukūʿ*.[284]

Mawlānā ʿAbd al-Ra'ūf Sindū said about this ḥadīth: "Ibn al-Sakan, Ibn al-Turkumānī and al-Albānī authenticated it. Imām Abū Dāwūd has a lengthy discussion on this ḥadīth. The summary of the discussion is that the additional words of *qunūt* before *rukūʿ* are rare (*shādh*). Imām al-Bayhaqī has also mentioned the discussion of Imām Abū Dāwūd. However, Ibn al-Turkumānī in *al-Jawhar al-Naqiyy* (3: 39-40) and al-Albānī in Irwā' al-Ghalīl (2: 167-168) have refuted him. Also, this ḥadīth has testimonial reports (*shawāhid*) from Ibn Masʿūd, Ibn ʿAbbās and Ibn ʿUmar ﷺ which state that Rasūlullāh ﷺ performed *qunūt* before *rukūʿ*."[285]

Regarding the narrations that mention *qunūt* after *rukūʿ*, Mawlānā ʿAbd al-Ra'ūf Sindū, Shaykh al-Albānī and Doctor Shafīq al-Raḥmān state that using these narrations as evidence for this issue is questionable, as these narrations are related to *qunūt nāzilah* (which is read in the fajr ṣalāh at times of difficulty), and they are not linked with the *qunūt* of witr. In the *qunūt* of witr, the supplication is established before *rukūʿ* from Rasūlullāh ﷺ.[286]

It should be noted that raising the hands when saying the *takbīr* before *qunūt* is also *sunnah*, as it is established from Sayyidunā ʿUmar, Sayyidunā Ibn Masʿūd, Sayyidunā Abū Hurayrah, and others amongst the Ṣaḥābah ﷺ (whose path Rasūlullāh ﷺ advised us to follow).[287]

---

284 *Nasā'ī* (1701); *Ibn Mājah* (1182)

285 *Al-Qawl al-Maqbūl*, p. 589.

286 *Al-Qawl al-Maqbūl*, p. 588; *Irwā' al-Ghalīl*, 2:163; *Namāz-i-Nabawī*, p. 236.

287 *Āthār al-Sunan*, pp. 230, 326.

Mawlānā ʿAbd al-Jabbār Ghaznawī (d. 1913 AH) writes: "Raising the hands in the supplication of *qunūt* is established from the Ṣaḥābah ﷺ and Tābiʿūn ﷺ."[288]

Imām al-Ṭaḥāwī ﷺ (d. 321 AH) said:

وَأَمَّا التَّكْبِيْرُ فِي الْقُنُوْتِ فِي الْوِتْرِ فَإِنَّهَا تَكْبِيْرَةٌ زَائِدَةٌ فِيْ تِلْكَ الصَّلٰوةِ، وَقَدْ أَجْمَعَ الَّذِيْنَ يَقْنُتُوْنَ قَبْلَ الرُّكُوْعِ عَلَى الرَّفْعِ مَعَهَا.

The *takbīr* in the *qunūt* of witr is an additional *takbīr* in the ṣalāh. Those who do *qunūt* before the *rukūʿ* have unanimously agreed that the hands will be raised.[289]

A final point to consider is that performing witr ṣalāh is compulsory (*wājib*), as Rasūlullāh ﷺ greatly emphasised performing it. Rasūlullāh ﷺ said:

الْوِتْرُ حَقٌّ، فَمَنْ لَّمْ يُوْتِرْ فَلَيْسَ مِنَّا.

Witr is established. Whoever does not perform witr is not amongst us.[290]

Ḥadīth 33
TWENTY *RAKʿAHS* OF TARĀWĪḤ IS *SUNNAH*

Tarāwīḥ ṣalāh is performed in Ramaḍān after the obligatory (*farḍ*) ṣalāh of ʿishā' and its *sunan*. Its *sunnah* number of *rakʿahs* is twenty. Sayyidunā ʿAbdullāh ibn ʿAbbās ﷺ reports:

أَنَّ رَسُوْلَ اللهِ ﷺ كَانَ يُصَلِّيْ فِيْ شَهْرِ رَمَضَانَ عِشْرِيْنَ رَكْعَةً وَّالْوِتْرَ.

288 *Fatāwā Ghaznawī*, p. 51; *Fatāwā ʿUlamā'-i-Ḥadīth*, 4:283.

289 *Sharḥ Maʿānī al-Āthār*, 1:455.

290 *Abū Dāwūd* (1416-1420)

Rasūlullāh ﷺ would perform twenty *rakʿahs* (tarāwīḥ) and witr.[291]

All the narrators of this ḥadīth are reliable, except for Ibrāhīm ibn ʿUthmān Abū Shaybah, the grandfather of Imām Abū Bakr ibn Abī Shaybah. He is not so weak as to cause this narration to be rejected.

Musnid al-Hind Imām Shāh ʿAbd al-ʿAzīz al-Muḥaddith al-Dihlawī (d. 1239 AH) said: "Imām al-Bayhaqī has weakened this ḥadīth on the basis that its narrator is the grandfather of Abū Bakr ibn Abī Shaybah, whereas the weakness in him is not such that it will render his narration abandoned (*matrūk*) altogether. However, if there is an authentic ḥadīth contradicting this ḥadīth, then it will be discarded."[292]

It is understood from this that there is no authentic narration contradicting this ḥadīth. The narration of Sayyidah ʿĀ'ishah ﷺ, which is presented against this ḥadīth, is related to tahajjud, not tarāwīḥ. There is a big difference between tahajjud and tarāwīḥ. Tarāwīḥ is specific to Ramaḍān, whilst tahajjud is performed all year round. Also, regardless of how weak this ḥadīth may be, due to the practice of Sayyidunā ʿUmar ﷺ and the Ummah, it will be credible as evidence.

Mawlānā Waḥīd al-Zamān said: "No one should assume that Sayyidunā ʿUmar ﷺ added something to the religion on his own part which he had no right to add, or that he gave the ruling of twenty *rakʿahs* based on his own opinion. Never! Allāh forbid that Sayyidunā ʿUmar ﷺ would do such a thing. Rather, he followed the prophetic method. In the era of Rasūlullāh ﷺ, everyone read behind one imām. Likewise, Sayyidunā ʿUmar ﷺ must have seen Rasūlullāh ﷺ performing twenty *rakʿahs*

291 *Muṣannaf Ibn Abī Shaybah*, 2:286; *al-Sunan al-Kubrā* 2:496.

292 *Fatāwā ʿAzīzī*, p. 484.

of tarāwīḥ, albeit the narration has not reached us with an authentic chain. Its chain contains Abū Shaybah Ibrāhīm ibn ʿUthmān whose narrations are censured (*munkar al-ḥadīth*). However, the era of Sayyidunā ʿUmar ﷺ was well before him. Hence, Sayyidunā ʿUmar ﷺ would have received the authentic narration, or witnessed it himself."[293]

Mawlānā Miyā Ghulām Rasūl writes: "The practice of the noble Ṣaḥābah ﷺ, the four Imāms and a large group of the Muslims, across the East and West, has been twenty-three *rakʿahs* (twenty tarāwīḥ and three witr) since the time of Sayyidunā ʿUmar ﷺ."[294]

In the *Muwaṭṭa'* of Imām Mālik, an authentic narration has been reported from Sayyidunā ʿUmar ﷺ (in the chapter: *bāb qiyām shahr ramaḍān*) that he instructed those who were reading tarāwīḥ on their own, or in small groups, to perform behind one imām in a large congregation, and he appointed Sayyidunā ʿUbayy ibn Kaʿb ﷺ as the imām of this congregation. Thereafter, there was a consensus (*ijmāʿ*) of the Ṣaḥābah ﷺ on twenty *rakʿahs* of tarāwīḥ.

Due to the instruction of Sayyidunā ʿUmar ﷺ and the consensus of the Ṣaḥābah ﷺ, no less than twenty *rakʿahs* of tarāwīḥ have been performed in the two Noble Ḥarams (al-Masjid al-Ḥarām and al-Masjid al-Nabawī) in congregation, from the era of Sayyidunā ʿUmar ﷺ until today.

For more detail, please refer to my book *Rakʿāt-i-Tarāwīḥ: Ek Taḥqīqī Jā'izah.*[295]

293 *Lughāt al-Ḥadīth*, p. 45.

294 *Yanābīʿ Tarjamah Risālah Tarāwīḥ*, p. 28.

295 This is a very detailed and comprehensive book written in Urdu, by Mawlānā Zahoor (may Allāh preserve him), on the topic of Tarāwīḥ. I pray to Allāh that it gets translated into English (Translator's Note).

Ḥadīth 34

IT IS PERMISSIBLE TO OFFER THE FAJR *SUNNAH* WHEN THE CONGREGATIONAL ṢALĀH HAS STARTED

It has been prohibited in ḥadīths to perform *sunnah* or *nafl* ṣalāh once the congregational ṣalāh has started. However, if one has not prayed the two *sunnah* of fajr ṣalāh and the congregational ṣalāh has started, he should first perform them in a corner of the mosque, or near the door, or behind a pillar,[296] if he knows he can then join the congregation and attain one *rakʿah*. This is because there is great emphasis on performing the *sunnah* of fajr, as mentioned in narrations, and Rasūlullāh ﷺ stressed their importance.

As for the ḥadīth which states it is impermissible to perform any ṣalāh, apart from the obligatory ṣalāh, once the *iqāmah* has started, the *sunnah* of fajr is an exception to this rule, as Rasūlullāh ﷺ himself allowed them.

Sayyidunā Abū Hurayrah رضي الله عنه reports from Rasūlullāh ﷺ:

إِذَا أُقِيْمَتِ الصَّلَوةُ فَلَا صَلَوةَ إِلَّا الْمَكْتُوْبَةَ، إِلَّا رَكْعَتَيِ الصُّبْحِ.

When the *iqāmah* is said for ṣalāh, there is no ṣalāh apart from the obligatory ṣalāh, except for the two *sunnah rakʿahs* of Fajr.[297]

Imām al-Bayhaqī criticised this narration due to two of its narrators: Ḥajjāj ibn al-Nuṣayr and ʿAbbād ibn Kathīr al-Ramalī. However, many hadith scholars (*muḥaddithūn*) also deemed them reliable. Imām al-ʿAjlī, Imām Ibn Ḥibbān and Imām Ibn Shāhīn have included Ḥajjāj amongst the authentic narrators. Imām Ibn Maʿīn has deemed him as a truthful (*ṣadūq*)

---

296 Essentially, where there is no disturbance caused to the congregation (Ed. note).

297 *Al-Sunan al-Kubrā*, 2:483.

shaykh.[298] Imām al-Ḥākim and Imām Abū Nuʿaym have used him for evidence in their *Ṣaḥīh* compilations.[299]

Also, great ḥadīth scholars (*muḥaddithūn*) like Imām Ibn Maʿīn, Imām ʿAlī ibn al-Madīnī, Imām Abū Bakr ibn Abī Shaybah, Imām Ibn Shāhīn, and others, have declared ʿAbbād reliable.[300]

Mawlānā Muḥammad Gawndlawī stated: "When a narrator's reliability is disputed, his ḥadīth is sound (*ḥasan*)."[301]

Therefore, the aforementioned ḥadīth is sound in the least. Also, it is supported by the practice of the Ṣaḥābah ﷡ and senior Tābiʿūn, as they would perform the fajr *sunnah* after the congregational ṣalāh had started, whereafter they would join the congregation.

The great Tābiʿī, Abū ʿUthmān al-Nahdī ﵀ said:

كُنَّا نَأْتِي عُمَرَ بْنَ الْخَطَّابِ ﵁ قَبْلَ أَنْ نُصَلِّيَ الرَّكْعَتَيْنِ قَبْلَ الصُّبْحِ، وَهُوَ فِي الصَّلَاةِ، فَنُصَلِّي الرَّكْعَتَيْنِ فِي آخِرِ الْمَسْجِدِ، ثُمَّ نَدْخُلُ مَعَ الْقَوْمِ فِي صَلَاتِهِمْ.

We (Ṣaḥābah and Tābiʿūn) would come to ʿUmar ibn al-Khaṭṭāb ﵁ (in al-Masjid al-Nabawī) before performing the two *rakʿahs* of *sunnah* before fajr, while he was leading ṣalāh. We would perform the two *rakʿahs* of *sunnah* at the back of the mosque, and then join the people in the congregational ṣalāh.[302]

Imām al-Ṭaḥāwī (d. 321 AH) reports the narration of Abū ʿUthmān with two different chains. In one of the chains, all its

298 *Tārīkh al-Thiqāt*, p. 109; *Kitāb al-Thiqāt*, 2:292; *Tarīkh Asmā' al-Thiqāt*, p. 11; *Mukhtaṣar al-Kāmil*, p. 247.

299 *Mustadrak al-Ḥākim* (4826); Abū Nuʿaym's *Al-Musnad al-Mustakhraj* (1676).

300 *Tarīkh ʿUthmān al-Dāramī*, p. 135; *Sawālāt ʿUthmān Ibn Abī Shaybah li ibn al-Madīnī*, p. 50; *Tarīkh Asmā' al-Thiqāt*, p. 231; *Tahdhīb al-Tahdhīb*, 3:70.

301 *Khayr al-Kalām*, p. 238.

302 *Sharḥ Maʿānī al-Āthār*, 1:258.

narrators are authentic and they are the narrators of *Ṣaḥīḥ al-Bukhārī*, except for Rawḥ ibn al-Faraj al-Qaṭṭān, who is very reliable and truthful.[303] Also, the narrator of the second chain is trustworthy and his narrations are sound.

It is clear from this narration that in the presence of a great Ṣaḥābī and righteous caliph, i.e., Sayyidunā ʿUmar ﷺ, the noble Ṣaḥābah ﷺ and great Tābiʿūn ﷺ would perform the two *rakʿāhs* of fajr after the congregational ṣalāh had already started, but Sayyidunā ʿUmar ﷺ did not censure them. Likewise, it was the practice of Sayyidunā ʿAbdullāh ibn ʿUmar ﷺ,[304] Sayyidunā ʿAbdullāh ibn Masʿūd ﷺ, Sayyidunā ʿAbdullāh ibn ʿAbbās ﷺ, Sayyidunā Abū 'l-Dardā' ﷺ and Sayyidunā Abū Mūsā al-Ashʿarī ﷺ that if the fajr ṣalāh had started but they had not yet performed their two *sunnah*, they would first read them in a corner of the mosque or behind a pillar, and then they would join the congregation.[305]

It should be understood by now that the ḥadīth that prohibits performing any ṣalāh when the congregational ṣalāh has started does not include the fajr *sunnah*, as they can be performed in a place away from the congregation, because Rasūlullāh ﷺ has permitted this. This is what the Ṣaḥābah ﷺ

303 *Tahdhīb al-Tahdhīb*, 2:175.

304 A non-muqallid scholar has mentioned a narration from *al-Sunan al-Kubrā* (2:483), reported by ʿAbdullāh ibn ʿUmar ﷺ that he had prohibited anyone performing *nafl* (*sunnah*) prayer during the *iqāmah*. However, this report has a narrator by the name of Ḥammād ibn Salamah, who according to this non-muqallid himself is weak (*Ḥāshiyah Juz' Rafʿ al-Yadayn*, p. 74; *al-Qawl al-Matīn*, p. 45). Hypothetically, if we consider this report to be authentic, in order to reconcile between the different narrations, the prohibition in this narration will be based on the scenario when one performs the two *rakʿahs* of *sunnah* in the rows of the congregational prayer.

305 *Sharḥ Maʿānī al-Āthār*, 1: 257-258; *Muṣannaf Ibn Abī Shaybah*, 2:153-154. *Muṣannaf ʿAbd al-Razzāq*, 2:294.

understood from the aforesaid ḥadīth and the narrations which greatly emphasise the importance of *sunnah* of fajr.

Mawlānā Nadhīr Ḥusayn al-Dihlawī (d. 1903 AD) writes: "If anyone performs the fajr *sunnah* in a place away from the mosque, whilst the congregation of the obligatory ṣalāh has started in the mosque, then this is a different matter whereupon one will not be taken to task."[306]

Ḥadīth 35

THE FAJR *SUNNAH* CAN BE OFFERED AFTER SUNRISE IF THEY ARE MISSED

If for some reason, one is unable to perform the fajr *sunnah* before the obligatory ṣalāh, one cannot perform them after the obligatory ṣalāh, but rather one will wait for the sun to rise fully and then perform them. This is established from the following ḥadīth in which Sayyidunā Abū Hurayrah ﷺ reports that Rasūlullāh ﷺ said:

مَنْ لَّمْ يُصَلِّ رَكْعَتَيِ الْفَجْرِ، فَلْيُصَلِّهِمَا بَعْدَ مَا تَطْلُعُ الشَّمْسُ.

Whoever does not perform thc two rakʿāhs of fajr should pray them after the sun has risen.[307]

Imām al-Ḥākim (d. 405 AH) and Ḥāfiẓ al-Dhahabī (d. 748 AH) deemed this ḥadīth authentic according to the criteria of Imām al-Bukhārī and Imām Muslim.[308] Imām Ibn Khuzaymah (d. 311 AH) and Imām Ibn Ḥibbān (d. 354 AH) have also reported

306 *Fatāwā Nadhīriyyah*, 1:433.

307 *Tirmidhī* (423); *Mustadrak al-Ḥākim* (1153)

308 *Mustadrak al-Ḥākim*, 1:451.

it in their ṣaḥīḥ compilations.[309] Shaykh al-Albānī also authenticated this ḥadīth.[310]

Some non-muqallids object to this ḥadīth due to its narrator Qatādah being a *mudallis*. However, this objection is invalid. As stated under ḥadīth twenty-one, quoting from the non-muqallid scholars, that the narrations of a *mudallis* in *Ṣaḥīḥ Ibn Ḥibbān* will be taken to be based on hearing (*samāʿ*). Also, the *tadlīs* of Qatādah is not harmful, because he only does *tadlīs* from trustworthy narrators, as clearly stated by Imām al-Ḥākim ؒ (d. 405 AH).[311] In addition, ʿAllāmah Ibn Ḥazm (d. 456 AH) has also regarded Qatādah's *tadlīs* to be unharmful.[312]

From this ḥadīth, we understand that if one does not perform the two *sunnah* of fajr before the obligatory ṣalāh, hc should not perform them immediately after the obligatory ṣalāh, but rather wait until the sun has completely risen.

This ḥadīth is also be supported by narrations in which Rasūlullāh ﷺ prohibited performing ṣalāh after fajr until the sun rises, as mentioned under ḥadīth nine.

❧

Ḥadīth 36
THERE IS NO *NAFL* ṢALĀH BEFORE MAGHRIB ṢALĀH

One will not perform any *nafl* ṣalāh between the *adhān* and *iqāmah* of maghrib, as Sayyidunā Buraydah ؓ narrates that Rasūlullāh ﷺ said:

309 *Ibn Khuzaymah* (1117); *Al-Iḥsān bi Tartīb Ṣaḥīḥ Ibn Ḥibbān* (2469).

310 *Silsilat al-Aḥādīth al-Ṣaḥīḥah* (2361).

311 *Maʿrifat ʿUlūm al-Ḥadīth,* p. 165.

312 *Iḥkām al-Aḥkām*, 1:137.

إِنَّ عِنْدَ كُلِّ أَذَانَيْنِ رَكْعَتَيْنِ، إِلَّا الْمَغْرِبَ.

There are two *rakʿahs* between every two calls (*adhān* and *iqāmah*), except for maghrib.[313]

This ḥadīth is authentic and all its narrators are trustworthy, including Ḥayyān ibn ʿUbaydullāh. Imām al-Bazzār, Imām Ibn al-Turkumānī and others have deemed him reliable and considered any objection against him to be insignificant.[314]

Imām al-Bazzār (d. 292 AH) in his *Musnad*, and Imām Ibn Shāhīn (d. 385 AH) in his book *Al-Nāsikh wa 'l-Mansūkh*, stated that the ḥadīth which permits two *rakʿahs* of *nafl* before maghrib ṣalāh is abrogated (*mansūkh*) due to the aforementioned ḥadīth.[315]

In addition to this, the aforesaid ḥadīth is further supported by the narration in which Sayyidunā ʿAbdullāh ibn ʿUmar ﵁ was asked about the two *rakʿahs* performed before the maghrib ṣalāh. He replied, "I did not see anyone in the time of Rasūlullāh ﷺ performing these two *rakʿahs*."[316] Similarly, there is a *mursal* narration of Imām Ibrāhīm al-Nakhaʿī (whose *mursal* narrations are authentic according to the ḥadīth experts)[317] in which he states: "Rasūlullāh ﷺ, Abū Bakr ﵁, ʿUmar ﵁ and ʿUthmān ﵁ would not perform these two *rakʿahs* before maghrib."[318]

ʿAllāmah al-Shawkānī (d. 1255 AH) has written:

وَلَمْ يَسْتَحِبَّهَا الْأَرْبَعَةُ الْخُلَفَاءُ ﵃، وَآخَرُوْنَ مِنَ الصَّحَابَةِ وَمَالِكٌ وَأَكْثَرُ الْفُقَهَاءِ.

313 *Al-Sunan al-Kubrā* 2:474; *al-Muʿjam al-Awsaṭ* (8338); *Musnad al-Bazzār*, (4422).

314 *Al-Baḥr al-Zakhkhār*, 10:303; *al-Jawhar al-Naqiyy*, 2:475-476.

315 *Maʿārif al-Sunan*, 2:143.

316 *Abū Dāwūd* (1284)

317 *Al-Istidhkār*, 8:13; *al-Tamhīd*, 1:55; *al-Mūqiẓah*, p. 40.

318 *Kitāb al-Āthār*, p. 48; *Muṣannaf ʿAbd al-Razzāq*, 2:289.

The four Caliphs, as well as other Ṣaḥābah ﷺ, Imām Mālik and the majority of the jurists did not consider the two rakʿāhs before maghrib to be laudable (*mustaḥabb*).[319]

❧

Ḥadīth 37
THE TIME FOR JUMUʿAH STARTS AFTER THE SUN'S MERIDIAN

Like ẓuhr ṣalāh, jumuʿah ṣalāh also starts after the sun's meridian, as this was the time when Rasūlullāh ﷺ would lead the ṣalāh. Sayyidunā Anas ibn Mālik ﷺ reports:

أَنَّ النَّبِيَّ ﷺ كَانَ يُصَلِّي الْجُمُعَةَ حِيْنَ تَمِيْلُ الشَّمْسُ

Nabī ﷺ would perform jumuʿah ṣalāh when the sun would move (after its meridian).[320]

It is clearly established from this ḥadīth that the time for jumuʿah ṣalāh starts after the sun's meridian, whereas there is no explicit, authentic ḥadīth which states it to start before the sun's meridian. According to Imām al-Bukhārī and the commentator of *Ṣaḥīḥ al-Bukhārī*, Ḥāfiẓ Ibn Ḥajar, the evidence for praying jumuʿah before the sun's meridian is weak.[321]

Mawlānā Mubārakpūrī (d. 1352 AH) said:

وَالظَّاهِرُ الْمُعَوَّلُ عَلَيْهِ هُوَ مَا ذَهَبَ إِلَيْهِ الْجُمْهُوْرُ؛ مِنْ أَنَّهُ لَا تَجُوْزُ الْجُمُعَةُ إِلَّا بَعْدَ زَوَالِ الشَّمْسِ، وَأَمَّا مَا ذَهَبَ إِلَيْهِ بَعْضُهُمْ مِنْ أَنَّهَا تَجُوْزُ قَبْلَ الزَّوَالِ، فَلَيْسَ فِيْهِ حَدِيْثٌ صَحِيْحٌ صَرِيْحٌ.

319 *Nayl al-Awṭār*, 1:239.

320 *Bukhārī* (904).

321 *Fatḥ al-Bārī*, 2:491.

> The apparent, relied upon opinion, which is adopted by the majority of the scholars, is that performing jumuʿah is only permissible after the sun's meridian. As for some of the scholars whose opinion is that it is permissible before the sun's meridian, there is no clear authentic ḥadīth regarding this.[322]

Mawlānā ʿAbd al-Jabbār Ghaznawī (d. 1331 AH) writes: "It is established from authentic ḥadīths, and the narrations of the four Caliphs and other noble Ṣaḥābah ﷺ, that the time of jumuʿah ṣalāh is after the sun's meridian. The narrations that suggest otherwise are either all weak or hold other possibilities, which cannot stand as evidence in front of the authentic narrations."[323] Also, according to the senior non-muqallidīn scholars, delivering the jumuʿah sermon (*khuṭbah*) before the sun's meridian is impermissible as is the case with jumuʿah ṣalāh."[324]

It should be noted that it is imperative (*wājib*) to listen to the Friday sermon before the ṣalāh, and it is prohibited to perform any ṣalāh during the sermon. The Messenger of Allāh ﷺ permitting a Ṣaḥābī to perform *nafl* during the sermon, as mentioned in a hadith, will be considered exclusive to that Ṣaḥābī.[325] This has also been acknowledged by some non-muqallid scholars.[326]

---

322 *Tuḥfat al-Aḥwadhī*, 1:361.

323 *Fatāwā ʿUlamā'-i-Ḥadīth*, 2:152.

324 Ibid, 1:175; *Maqālāt Rāshidiyyah*, 1:413.

325 *ʿUmdat al-Qārī*, 6:332-340.

326 *Fatāwā ʿUlamā'-i-Ḥadīth*, 2:154.

Ḥadīth 38
JUMUʿAH AND ʿĪD ṢALĀH ARE ONLY PERMISSIBLE IN A CITY

The jumuʿah and ʿīd ṣalāh are only permissible in a city, or in a big village which has the facilities of a city, as such a village will come under the ruling of a city. However, in normal villages, performing the jumuʿah and ʿīd ṣalāh will not be permissible, as established from the following narration: the great Tābiʿī, Abū ʿAbd al-Raḥmān al-Sulamī, reports from Sayyidunā ʿAlī ؓ that he said:

لَاتَشْرِيْقَ وَلَا جُمُعَةَ، إِلَّا فِيْ مِصْرٍ جَامِعٍ.

ʿĪd and jumuʿah is only in a big city.[327]

ʿAllāmah Ibn Ḥazm al-Ẓāhirī (d. 456 AH) authenticated this ḥadīth.[328]

Ḥāfiẓ Badr al Dīn al-ʿAynī (d. 855 AH) and Ḥāfiẓ Ibn Ḥajar al-ʿAsqalānī (d. 852 AH) authenticated the chain of this ḥadīth, and they wrote in its commentary:

وَمَعْنَاهُ لَاصَلَاةَ جُمُعَةٍ وَلَاصَلَاةَ عِيْدٍ.

The meaning of this ḥadīth is that there is no ṣalāh of jumuʿah or ʿīd (except in a big city).[329]

This ḥadīth is transmitted as *marfūʿ*, i.e., Sayyidunā ʿAli ؓ narrates it from Rasūlullāh ﷺ, and also as a *mawqūf* ḥadīth of Sayyidunā ʿAli ؓ. Although most of the ḥadīth scholars (*muḥaddithūn*) have reported it as halted (*mawqūf*),[330] it will

327 *Muṣannaf Ibn Abī Shaybah*, 2:10; *al-Sunan al-Kubrā*, 2:177.

328 *Al-Muḥallā*, 5:38.

329 *ʿUmdat al-Qārī*, 6:418; *al-Dirāyah*, 1:214; *Fatḥ al-Bārī*, 2:581.

330 A narration which is attributed to a Ṣaḥābī.

come under the ruling of a raised (*marfū*ʿ) ḥadīth, because it is a matter that is not related to one's own opinion or analogy (*qiyās*). A statement of a Ṣaḥābī that cannot be based on personal opinion or analogy will be deemed as *marfū*ʿ, as he must have heard it from Rasūlullāh ﷺ. Even if this narration is regarded only as *mawqūf*, it will still qualify as evidence, as it is the statement of Sayyidunā ʿAlī ؓ, one of the righteous Caliphs by consensus, and whose *sunnah* Rasūlullāh ﷺ ordered us to follow, like his own *sunnah.*[331]

In conclusion, the aforementioned ḥadīth can be used as evidence in all circumstances, especially when there is no contradicting narration stating the permissibility of praying jumuʿah in normal villages.

❧

Ḥadīth 39
THERE ARE FOUR *TAKBĪRS* IN ʿĪD ṢALĀH AS IN JANĀZAH ṢALĀH,

Just as there are four *takbīrs* in janāzah ṣalāh, there are four *takbīrs* in each *rakʿah* of ʿīd al-fiṭr and ʿīd al-aḍḥā ṣalāh. In the first *rakʿah*, there are four *takbīrs* including the opening *takbīr taḥrīmah* before the recitation (*qirā'ah*), and in the second *rakʿah* there are four *takbīrs*, including the *takbīr* for *rukū*ʿ after the recitation. Besides the *takbīr taḥrīmah* and the *takbīr* for *rukū*ʿ, the remaining six *takbīrs* are known as additional (*zā'id*) *takbīrs*.

The Prophet ﷺ would perform only six additional *takbīrs* in the two ṣalāhs of ʿīd, as it is reported by Abū ʿĀ'ishah ؒ, the companion of Sayyidunā Abū Hurayrah ؓ:

---

331 *Tirmidhī* (2676).

أَنَّ سَعِيْدَ بْنَ الْعَاصِ رضي الله عنه سَأَلَ أَبَا مُوْسَى الْأَشْعَرِيَّ رضي الله عنه وَحُذَيْفَةَ ابْنَ الْيَمَانِ رضي الله عنه: كَيْفَ كَانَ رَسُوْلُ اللهِ ﷺ يُكَبِّرُ فِي الْأَضْحَى وَالْفِطْرِ؟ فَقَالَ أَبُوْ مُوْسَى: كَانَ يُكَبِّرُ أَرْبَعًا تَكْبِيْرَهُ عَلَى الْجَنَائِزِ. فَقَالَ حُذَيْفَةُ: صَدَقَ. فَقَالَ أَبُوْ مُوسَى: كَذَلِكَ كُنْتُ أُكَبِّرُ فِيْ الْبَصْرَةِ حَيْثُ كُنْتُ عَلَيْهِمْ: قَالَ أَبُوْ عَائِشَةَ: وَأَنَا حَاضِرٌ سَعِيْدَ بْنَ الْعَاصِ.

Saʿīd ibn al-ʿĀṣ رضي الله عنه asked Abū Mūsā al-Ashʿarī رضي الله عنه and Ḥudhaifah ibn al-Yamān رضي الله عنه: "How would Rasūlullāh ﷺ say the *takbīr* in the ṣalāh of the day of sacrifice (al-aḍḥā) and of the breaking of the fast (al-fiṭr)?" Abū Mūsā رضي الله عنه replied: "He said the *takbīr* four times as he did at funerals." Hudhaifah رضي الله عنه said: "He is correct." Then Abū Mūsā said: "I used to say the *takbīr* in a similar way when I was the governor of Baṣrah." Abū ʿĀ'ishah said: "I was present there when Saʿīd ibn al-ʿĀṣ رضي الله عنه asked."[332]

Shaykh al-Albānı has stated that all narrators of this ḥadīth are trustworthy, except for Abū ʿĀ'ishah, regarding whom Ḥāfiẓ Ibn Ḥajar said that his narration is accepted in the presence of supporting evidence. Because this ḥadīth reported by him is supported by numerous authentic narrations, it will be sound and credible as evidence.[333]

The method of ʿīd ṣalāhs and the *takbīrs* therein has been explained by Sayyidunā ʿAbdullāh ibn Masʿūd رضي الله عنه, in the presence of Sayyidunā Ḥudhaifah and Sayyidunā Abū Mūsā al-Ashʿarī رضي الله عنهم: Firstly, one will start the ṣalāh by saying the *takbīr taḥrīmah*, then (after *thanā'*) say the three *takbīrs* and recite (*qirā'ah*), then perform *rukūʿ* whilst saying the *takbīr*, then make *sajdah*, then (after completing the two *sajdahs*, he should

332 *Abū Dāwūd* (1153); *Sharḥ Maʿānī al-Āthār*, 2:439; Ṭabarānī's *Musnad al-Shāmiyyīn* (3570).

333 *Silsilat al-Aḥādīth al-Ṣaḥīḥah* (2997).

say the *takbīr* and) stand up and recite, then (after completing the recitation) say the three *takbīrs*, and then make *rukūʿ* whilst saying the *takbīr* (then complete the ṣalāh as normal). Upon hearing this, Sayyidunā Ḥudhayfah and Sayyidunā Abū Mūsā al-Ashʿarī ﷺ said: "Abū ʿAbd al-Raḥmān (ʿAbdullāh ibn Masʿūd ﷺ) has spoken the truth."[334]

Ḥāfiẓ Ibn Ḥajar al-ʿAsqalānī and Shaykh al-Albānī said that the chain of this narration is authentic.[335] Mawlānā ʿAbd al-Raḥmān Mubārakpūrī also acknowledged the authenticity of this narration.[336]

Under ḥadīth thirty-two, it was discussed that Imām al-Ṭaḥāwī stated a consensus (*ijmāʿ*) of the scholars that the hands will be raised with the additional *takbīrs* of ṣalāh. Based on this, it will be preferable to raise the hands with the six additional *takbīrs* of ʿīd ṣalāh. In addition to this, Mawlānā Sharaf al-Dīn al-Dihlawī states that raising the hands in the *takbīrs* of ʿīd ṣalāh is established from Sayyidunā Ibn ʿUmar ﷺ, and it has been the practice of ḥadīth scholars (*muḥaddithūn*) for centuries. Hence, it is worthy of acting upon.[337]

Ḥadīth 40
THERE IS NO *QIRĀ'AH* IN JANĀZAH ṢALĀH

As mentioned in the previous hadith, there are four *takbīrs* in janāzah ṣalāh. After the first *takbīr*, *thanā'* will be read; after the second *takbīr*, blessings (*ṣalawāt*) will be sent on

334 *Sharḥ Maʿānī al-Āthār*, 2:438.

335 *Al-Dirāyah*, 1:220; *Silsilat al-Aḥādīth al-Ṣaḥīḥah* (2997).

336 *Maqālāt Mubārakpūrī*, p. 234.

337 *Fatāwā ʿUlamā'-i-Ḥadīth*, 3:156.

Rasūlullāh ﷺ; after the third *takbīr,* supplication will be made for the deceased and the believers; and after the fourth *takbīr, salām* will be said both to the right and left.

Sūrat al-Fātiḥah, or another *sūraḥ*, will not be read as recitation (*qirā'ah*) after any of the four *takbīrs*.

Sayyidunā ʿAbdullāh ibn Masʿūd narrates:

لَمْ يُوَقِّتْ لَنَا فِى الصَّلَاةِ عَلَى الْمَيِّتِ قِرَاءَةً وَّلَا قَوْلٌ.

There was no recitation or any specific words fixed for us (by Rasūlullāh ﷺ) in janāzah ṣalāh.[338]

Ḥāfiẓ Nūr al-Dīn al-Haythamī (d. 807 AH) said: "The narrators of this ḥadīth are the narrators of Ṣaḥīḥ al-Bukhārī."[339]

Imām al-Ṭabarānī (d. 360 AH) has narrated the report of Sayyidunā ʿAbdullāh ibn Masʿūd with two chains: the first of them is sound in itself (*ḥasan li dhātihī*), and the second is sound due to other narrations (*ḥasan li ghayrihī*).[340] The *tadlīs* of Sharīk al-Nakhaʿī, who is one of its narrators, is unharmful, as acknowledged by the non-muqallid scholars, and as is understood from Mawlānā Mubārakpūrī under ḥadīth twenty-one, especially when there are narrations from trustworthy narrators like Abū Ḥamzā al-Sukkarī and others to support his narration. Imām al-Dāraquṭnī (d. 385 AH) deemed this ḥadīth as preserved (*maḥfūẓ*) after writing a lengthy discussion on it.[341]

It is clear from the abovementioned ḥadīth that there is no recitation in janāzah ṣalāh, neither of *Sūrat al-Fātiḥah* nor any other *sūrah*. This is the opinion of the majority of the noble Ṣaḥābah , amongst them: Sayyidunā ʿUmar , Sayyidunā

338 *Musnad Aḥmad ibn Ḥanbal*: quoted from *Majmaʿ al-Zawā'id*: 3:32.

339 Ibid.

340 *Al-Muʿjam al-Kabīr* (9604, 9606).

341 *Kitāb al-ʿIlal* (867).

ʿAlī ﷺ,[342] Sayyidunā ʿAbdullāh ibn ʿUmar ﷺ,[343] Sayyidunā Faḍālah ibn ʿUbayd ﷺ,[344] Sayyidunā Abū Hurayrah ﷺ,[345] Sayyidunā Jābir ibn ʿAbdullāh ﷺ and Sayyidunā Wāthilah ibn al-Asqaʿ ﷺ.

Imām Mālik ﷺ said: "This is not practiced (i.e., recitation in janāzah ṣalāh) in our city (al-Madīnah al-Munawwrah). Janāzah ṣalāh is only a supplication (*duʿā'*), and I found the people of knowledge in my city following this."[346]

However, because *Sūrat al-Fātiḥah* consists of Allāh's praise and glorification, if someone says it as a supplication and not as recitation, it will be permissible.

It should be noted that in the four *takbīrs* of janāzah ṣalāh, the hands will only be raised with the first *takbīr*, as it is established that Rasūlullāh ﷺ only raised his hands in the first *takbīr* of janāzah ṣalāh.[347] This has also been acknowledged by senior non-muqallid scholars: ʿAllāmah Ibn Ḥazm, ʿAllāmah al-Shawkānī, ʿAllāmah Waḥīd al-Zamān, Mawlānā Mubārakpūrī, Shaykh al-Albānī, and others.[348]

As with normal ṣalāh, janāzah ṣalāh will have two *salāms* after the fourth *takbīr*, and this is established from ḥadīths of Rasūlullāh ﷺ which are authenticated by Imām al-Nawawī and others,[349] alongside Shaykh al-Albānī.[350] Mawlānā Muḥammad Ismāʿīl Salafī writes that one should make *salām* to both sides at the end of janāzah ṣalāh.[351]

---

342 *Muṣannaf Ibn Abī Shaybah*, 3:179.

343 *Muwaṭṭa'* (535).

344 *Muṣannaf Ibn Abī Shaybah*, 3:182.

345 *Muwaṭṭa'* (533); *Maqālāt Mubārakpūrī*, p. 307.

346 *Al-Mudawwanat al-Kubrā*, 1:158-159.

347 *Sunan al-Dāraquṭnī*, 2:93.

348 *Al-Muḥallā*, 5:1121; *Nayl al-Awṭār*, 1:758; *Nuzul al-Abrār*, 1:174; *Maqālāt Mubārakpūrī*, p. 310; *Aḥkām al-Janā'iz*, p. 147-148.

349 *Al-Sunan al-Kubrā*, 4:43.

350 *Aḥkām al-Janā'iz*, p. 162.

351 *Rasūl-i-Akram ﷺ kī Namāz*, p. 133.

One should remember that the janāzah ṣalāh will be performed outside the masjid in a specific, designated place, as Rasūlullāh ﷺ prohibited it inside the Masjid.[352]

Mawlānā Mubārakpūrī writes, "Janāzah ṣalāh should not be habitually performed inside the masjid, but rather there should be a designated place for it outside the masjid, just as in the time of Rasūlullāh ﷺ there was a specific place allocated for it outside al-Masjid al-Nabawī ﷺ."[353]

Also, janāzah ṣalāh of an absent deceased person is not legislated, as acknowledged by non-muqallid scholars, and to use the incident of Najāshī ﵀ as evidence will be incorrect, as this was exclusive to him.[354]

ربنا تقبل منا إنك أنت السميع العليم، وصلى الله تعالى على خير خلقه محمد وعلى آله وأصحابه وعلى من اتبعهم بإحسان إلى يوم الدين، برحمتك يا أرحم الراحمين.

Our Lord, accept from us. Indeed, it is You who are All-Hearing, All-Knowing.
May Allah bless the best of His creation, Muḥammad, his family, his Companions, and those who follow them in excellence until the Day of Recompense. Accept, through Your mercy, O Most Merciful of those who show mercy.

(Mawlānā) Zahoor Ahmad al-Husayni
May Allāh forgive him
22 RABĪʿ AL-THĀNĪ 1428 AH | THURSDAY 10 MAY 2007

352 *Sharḥ Maʿānī al-Āthār*, 1:331.
353 *Maqālāt Mubārakpūrī*, p. 302-303.
354 *Al-Qawl al-Maqbūl*, p. 714-717.

BIBLIOGRAPHY

Full details of the precise editions were not available to the translator, and hence detailed information has not been provided. Some of the works listed in the bibliography have been added by the editor.

ʿAbd al-Barr, Yūsuf ibn ʿAbdullāh ibn. *Al-Tamhīd*

Jāmiʿ Bayān al-ʿIlm

Al-Istidhkār

Al-Muntaqā

ʿAjlī, Aḥmad ibn ʿAbdullāh. *Tārīkh al-Thiqāt*

ʿAlī Zai, Zubair. *Al-Qawl al-Matīn*

Ḥāshiyah Juz' Rafʿ al-Yadayn

ʿAsqalānī, Shihāb al-Dīn Ibn Ḥajar. *Bulūgh al-Marām*

Al-Nukat ʿalā Kitāb Ibn al-Ṣalāḥ

Natā'ij al-Afkār

Tahdhīb al-Tahdhīb

Talkhīṣ al-Ḥabīr

Taqrīb al-Tahdhīb

Al-Maṭālib al-ʿAliyah

Fatḥ al-Bārī

Tabṣīr al-Muntabih

ʿAyni, Badr al-Dīn. *ʿUmdat al-Qārī*

ʿAẓīmābādī, Shams al-Ḥaqq. *ʿAwn al-Maʿbūd*

Albānī, Nāṣir al-Dīn. *Aḥkām al-Adhān wa'l-Iqāmah*

Aḥkām al-Janā'iz

Irwā' al-Ghalīl

Silsilat al-Aḥādīth al-Ṣaḥīḥah

Al-Ḥāwī min Fatāwā al-Shaykh al-Albānī

Ṣifat Ṣalāt al-Nabīyy

Anas, Mālik ibn. *Al-Mudawwanat al-Kubrā*

Muwaṭṭa'

Aṣbahānī, Abū Nuʿaym Aḥmad bin ʿAbdullāh. *Al-Musnad al-Mustakhraj ʿalā Ṣaḥīḥ Muslim*

Maʿrifat al-Ṣaḥābah

Aṣbahānī, Abū Nuʿaym. *Musnad al-Imām Abī Ḥanīfah*

Atharī, Irshād al-Haq. *Maqālāt*

Tawḍīḥ al-Kalām

Baghawī, Ḥusayn. *Maṣābīḥ al-Sunnah*

Baghdādī, Aḥmad ibn Manīʿ. *Musnad Aḥmad ibn Manīʿ*

Bahujiyānī, ʿAṭā ullah Hanīf. *Al-Taʿlīqāt al-Salafiyyah*

Bayhaqi, Abū Bakr Aḥmad ibn Ḥusayn. *Al-Sunan al-Kubrā*

Bayqūnī, ʿUmar. *Al-Manẓūmah al-Bayqūniyyah*

Bazzār, Abū Bakr. *Al-Baḥr al-Zakhkhār*

Musnad al-Bazzār

Bhopālī, Nawāb Siddīq Ḥasan Khān. *Al-Rawḍat al-Nadiyyah*

Itḥāf al-Nubalā'

Bukhārī, Muḥammad ibn Ismāʿīl. *Ṣaḥiḥ al-Bukhārī*

Al-Adab al-Mufrad

Būṣīrī, Aḥmad b. Ismā'īl. *Itḥāf al-Khiyarat al-Maharah*

Dāraquṭnī, ʿAli ibn ʿUmar. *Sunan al-Dāraquṭnī*

Kitāb al-ʿIlal

Dārimī, ʿUthmān ibn Saʿīd. *Tarīkh ʿUthmān ibn Saʿīd al-Dārimī*

Sunan al-Dārimī

Dhahabī, Shams al-Dīn Muḥammad ibn Aḥmad. T*adhkirat al-Ḥuffāẓ*

al-Mūqiẓah

Dihlawī, ʿAbd al-Azīz. *Fatāwā ʿAzīzī*

Dihlawī, Nadhīr. *Fatāwā Nadhīriyyah*

Dihlawī, Shāh Walī'ullāh. *Kalimāt Ṭayyibāt*

Ḥujjatullāh al-Bālighah

Dakkanī, Waḥīd al-Zamān. *Kanz al-Ḥaqā'iq*

Lughāt al-Ḥadīth

Faisal, Ilyās. *Namāz-i-Payambar*
Ghaznawī, ʿAbd al-Jabbār. *Fatāwā Ghaznawī*
Gawndlawī, Muḥammad. *Al-Taḥqīq al-Rāsikh*
Khayr al-Kalām
Ḥanbal, Ahmad ibn. *Musnad Aḥmad*
Ḥārithī, ʿAbdullāh ibn Muḥammad. *Musnad Abī Ḥanīfah*
Ḥarrāni, Aḥmad ibn Taymiyyah. *Minhāj al-Sunnah*
Ḥasan, Nur al-. *Fatḥ al-ʿAllām*
ʿArf al-Jādī
Ḥaṣkafī, Ṣadr 'l-Dīn Mūsā ibn Zakariyyā. *Musnad al-Imām al-Aʿẓam*
Haythamī, ʿAli ibn Abī Bakr. *Majmaʿ al-Zawā'id*
Ḥazm, ʿAlī ibn Aḥmad ibn. *Al-Muḥallā*
Iḥkām fī al-uṣūl al-Aḥkām
Ḥumayd, ʿAbd ibn. *Musnad ʿAbd ibn Ḥumayd*
Ḥumaydī, Abū Bakr ʿAbdullāh ibn Zubayr. *Musnad al-Ḥumaydī*
Ḥusayni, Zahoor Ahmad. *Imām Aʿẓam Abū Ḥanīfah ka Muḥaddithānah Maqām*
Rakʿāt-i-Tarāwīḥ: Ek Taḥqīqī Jā'izah
Ibn Abī Shaybah, ʿUthmān. *Suwālāt ʿUthmān Ibn Abī Shaybah li ibn al-Madīnī*
Ibn al-Jawzī, ʿAbd al-Raḥmān. *Al-La'ālī al-Maṣnūʿah*
Ibn al-Mundhir, Abū Bakr. *Al-Awsaṭ*
Ibn Ḥibbān, Abū Ḥātim. *Al-Iḥsān bi-Tartīb Ṣaḥīh Ibn Ḥibbān*
Kitāb al-Thiqāt
Tarīkh Aṣbahān
Isfarāyīnī, Abū ʿAwānah Yaʿqūb ibn Isḥāq. *Ṣaḥīḥ Abī ʿAwānah*
Karmī, Marʿī ibn Yūsuf. *Dalīl al-Ṭālib*
Kathīr, Ismāʿīl ibn ʿUmar ibn. *Al-Bidāyah wa 'l-Nihāyah*
Khaldūn, ʿAbd al-Raḥmān ibn Muḥammad ibn. *Muqaddamah ibn Khaldūn*
Khawārizmī, Muḥammad ibn Maḥmūd. *Jāmiʿ al-Masānīd*

Khuzaymah, Abū Bakr Muḥammad ibn Isḥāq ibn. *Ṣaḥīḥ ibn Khuzaymah.*
Makkī, ʿAli ibn Sulṭan. *Dhayl al-Jawāhir*
Makkī, Al-Muwaffaq ibn Ahmad. *Manāqib Abī Ḥanīfah,*
Makkī, Shīhāb al-Dīn Aḥmad ibn Ḥajr al-Haythamī. *Al-Khayrāt al-Ḥisān*
Makkī, ʿAbd al-Ḥafīẓ. *Istiḥbāb al-Duʿā' Baʿd al-Farā'iḍ wa Rafʿ al-Yadayn Fīhi*
Mā'kūlā, ʿAlī ibn. *Al-Ikmāl*
Maqrīzī, Aḥmad ibn ʿAli. *Mukhtaṣar al-Kāmil*
Mārdīnī, Ibn Turkumānī. *Al-Jawhar al-Naqiyy*
Maqdisī, Ḍiyā al-Dīn. *Al-Aḥādīth al-Mukhtārah*
Maqdisī, Muḥammad ibn Aḥmad. *Al-Mukhtaṣar Fī Ṭabaqāt ʿUlamā al-ḥadīth*
Mūṣīlī, Abū Yaʿlā Aḥmad ibn ʿAli. *Musnad Abī Yaʿlā*
Mian, Ghulām Rasūl. *Yanābīʿ Tarjamah Risālah Tarāwīḥ*
Mubārakpūrī, Muḥammad ʿAbd al-Raḥmān. *Taḥqīq al-Kalām*
Ibkār al-Minan
Maqālāt Mubārakpūrī
Tuḥfat al-Aḥwadhī
Sīrat al-Bukhārī
Mundhirī, ʿAbd al-Aẓīm ibn ʿAbd al-Qawī. *Mukhtaṣar Sunan Abī Dāwūd*
Najdī, Muḥammad ibn ʿAbd al-Wahhāb. *Mu'allafāt al-Shaykh Muḥammad ibn ʿAbd al-Wahhāb*
Nasā'ī, Aḥmad ibn Shuaʿyb. *Sunan al- Nasā'ī*
Naysābūrī, Muslim ibn al-Ḥajjaj. *Ṣaḥīḥ al-Muslim*
Nawawī, Yaḥya ibn Sharaf. *Sharḥ al-Muhadhdhab*
Nīmawī, Muḥammad ibn ʿAlī. *Āthār al-Sunan*
Nīshāpūrī, Muḥammad ibn ʿAbdullāh al-Hākim. *Maʿrifat ʿUlūm al-Ḥadīth*
Qasṭalānī, Aḥmad ibn Muḥammad. *Irshād al-Sārī*

Qurashī, ʿAbd al-Qādir ibn Muḥammad. *Al-Jawāhir al-Muḍī'ah*
Rashīdī, Badīʿ al-Dīn. *Maqālāt Rāshidiyyah*
Rawparī, ʿAbdullāh. *Fatāwā Aḥl-i-Ḥadīth*
Risālah Rafʿ Yadayn Aur Āmīn
Sakhāwī, Shams al-Dīn Muḥammad ibn ʿAbd al-Raḥmān. *Fatḥ al-Mughīth*
Salafī, Ismāʿīl. *Rasūl-i-Akram* ﷺ *kī Namāz*
Ṣāliḥī, Muḥammad ibn Yūsuf. *ʿUqūd al-Jumān fī Manāqib al-Imām al-Aʿẓam Abī Ḥanīfah al-Nuʿmān*
Ṣanʿāni, Muḥammad ibn Ismāʿīl. *Subūl al-Salām*
Ṣanʿānī, ʿAbd al-Razzāq. *Muṣannaf ʿAbd al-Razzāq*
Sayswānī, Bashīr al-Dīn. *Al-Burhān al-ʿUjāb*
Saʿīdī, ʿAlī Muḥammad. *Fatāwā ʿUlamā'-i-Ḥadīth*
Shāhīn, ʿUmar ibn. *Tarīkh Asmā' al-Thiqāt*
Shāhjahānpūrī, Abū Yaḥya. *Al-Irshād ilā Sabīl al-Rashād*
Shākir, Aḥmad. *Al-Bāʿith al-Ḥathīth*
Shāmī, Ibn ʿĀbidīn. *Radd al-Muḥtār*
Shawkānī, Muḥammad ibn ʿAlī. *Nayl al-Awṭār*
Rasā'il Dīniyyah Salafiyyah
Shaybah, Abū Bakr ibn Abī. *Muṣannaf ibn Abī Shaybah*
Shaybānī, Muḥammad ibn Ḥasan. *Kitāb al-Āthār*
Kitāb al-Ḥujjah ʿalā Ahl al-Madīnah
Sijistānī, Abū Dāwūd. *Sunan Abī Dāwūd*
Marāsīl Abī Dāwūd
Sindhi, Muḥammad Ḥāshim. *Tarṣīʿ al-Durrah Maʿa Dirham al-Ṣurrah*
Sindhū, ʿAbd al-Ra'uf. *Al-Qawl al-Maqbūl*
Siyālkawtī, Muḥammad Ibrāhīm Mīr. *Tārīkh Ahl-i-Ḥadīth*
Siyālkawtī, Muḥammad Ṣādiq. *Ṣalāt al-Rasūl*
Siyālkawtī, Shafīq al-Raḥmān. *Namāz-i-Nabawī*
Suyūṭī, Jalāl al-Dīn. *Ṭabaqat al-Ḥuffaz*
Tabyīḍ al-Ṣaḥīfah
Faḍḍ al-Wiʿā'

Ṭabarānī, Sulaymān ibn Aḥmad. *Al-Muʿjam al-Kabīr*
Kitāb al-Duʿā'
Musnad al-Shāmiyyīn
Tabrīzī, Muḥammad ibn ʿAbdullāh Khaṭīb. *Mishkāt al-Maṣābīḥ*
Ṭaḥāwi, Abū Jaʿfar Aḥmad ibn Muḥammad. *Sharḥ Maʿānī al-Āthār*
Thanā'ullāh, Amritsarī. *Fatāwā Thanā'iyyah*
Tirmidhī, Abū ʿĪsā Muḥammad ibn ʿĪsā. *Jāmiʿ at-Tirmidhī*
Wazīr, Muḥammad ibn Ibrāhīm. *Al-Rawḍ al-Bāsim fī 'l-Dhabb ʿan Sunnat Abī 'l-Qāsim*
Zamān, Waḥīd. *Nuzul al-Abrār*
Zarqānī, Muḥammad ibn ʿAbd al-Bāqī. *Sharḥ al-Zarqānī ʿalā al-Manẓūmah al Bayqūniyyah*
Zaydī, Shafīʿ al-Raḥmān. *Ṣalāt al-Nabiyy*
Zaylaʿī, Jamāl al-Dīn ʿAbdullāh. *Naṣb al-Rāyah*